THE CASTLE LECTURES IN ETHICS,

POLITICS, AND ECONOMICS

The Democratic Faith

Essays on Democratic Citizenship

PAUL M. SNIDERMAN

Yale

UNIVERSITY PRESS

New Haven and London

Published with assistance from the foundation established in memory of James Wesley Cooper of the Class of 1865, Yale College.

Yale University Press books may be purchased in quantity for educational, business, or promotional use. For information, please e-mail sales.press@yale.edu (U.S. office) or sales@yaleup.co.uk (U.K. office).

Set in Janson Roman and Monotype Van Dijck types by Tseng Information Systems, Inc.
Printed in the United States of America.

Library of Congress Control Number: 2016957556
ISBN 978-0-300-19709-9 (hardcover : alk. paper)

A catalogue record for this book is available from the British Library.

This paper meets the requirements of ANSI/NISO Z39.48-1992 (Permanence of Paper).

10 9 8 7 6 5 4 3 2 1

Parts of this book were given as the Castle Lectures in Yale's Program in Ethics, Politics, and Economics, delivered by Paul M. Sniderman in 2014.

The Castle Lectures were endowed by Mr. John K. Castle. They honor his ancestor the Reverend James Pierpont, one of Yale's original founders. Given by established public figures, Castle Lectures are intended to promote reflection on the moral foundations of society and government and to enhance understanding of ethical issues facing individuals in our complex modern society.

For Suz
My partner, my lifeline

Contents

Acknowledgments

I thank Nicholas Sambanis, acting on behalf of Yale's Program in Ethics, Politics, and Economics, for the invitation to give the 2014 Castle Lectures in Ethics, Politics, and Economics. Endowed by John K. Castle to honor his ancestor the Reverend James Pierpont, one of Yale's original founders, an objective of the Castle Lectures is "to promote reflection on the moral foundations of society and government." This was an exceptional honor; still more, an exceptional opportunity.

This book, I fear, has a big obstacle to overcome. A sign of being savvy in the study of public opinion is a readiness to acknowledge the limitations of citizens, to own up to how little they know about politics, how fitfully they pay attention to it, how sporadically they think about it, how haphazardly they put together their ideas about it. I accept all this, pretty much, yet I present results suggesting that citizens are much better at making coherent political choices than previous research has concluded. Better, I must emphasize, is not the same as excellent, and the politically ambitious being as clever as they are, there are drawbacks as well as advantages to being coherent. All the same, this is a more upbeat account than is usually on offer. May I say in my defense that the view of politics that underpins this account faces up more squarely than is customary to the foundational role of conflict and the contestability of claims to knowledge and values in a democratic politics?

I have many to thank. Once again, I have had the benefit of a manuscript passing through Martin Shapiro's logical X-ray-machine mind. Antoine Banks, Ryan Enos, Paul Goren, Bob Huckfeldt, Gabe Lenz, and Eric Schickler read all or big parts. Yphtach Lelkes made an indispensable contribution to my thinking about ideology in mass publics. Rune Slothuus read the manuscript again, and again, and if I have kept an accurate count, yet again, each time providing detailed, constructive suggestions for improvement. His encouragement matched his suggestions. John Bullock was, as always, a model of thoughtfulness.

I owe debts of unique depth to five—unique in my experience at least. Edward Carmines has been a partner for a bit more than twenty-five years now. The analysis in Chapter 3 grew out of our joint work, yet he has allowed me to take credit alone. Generosity is only one of his outstanding qualities. Then, notwithstanding the critical stance that I take toward their work, Christopher Achen, Larry Bartels, Stanley Feldman, and John Zaller, writing as friends, helped me see more clearly some of the strengths of their work that I had not properly appreciated and some of the weakness of mine that I had not clearly recognized. In addition, John spent days, possibly the larger part of several weeks, recovering code analysis and helping in every way in my replication of his results. He is a model of the scientist.

As always, Richard Juster has provided a standard for analysis; as always, I have fallen short, but thanks to him, I have at least fallen in the right direction. At Stanford, I once again have Karen Cook and Chris Thomsen, director and executive director of the Institute for Research in the Social Sciences, respectively, to thank for material and collegial help. In addition, for collegial readings, there are Eamonn Callan, Andrew Hall, Clayton Nall, and Rob Reich. I could not have done the reanalysis of the Zaller-Feldman data without Nick Eubank. He is a marvel of exactness and clarity. Matthew Tyler helped me over the finish line, thanks to his acuity in reading the manuscript. Stephen Haber, Jackie Sargent, and Eliana Vasquez are, quite simply, my support system at Stanford. I owe them many productive days and even more happy ones. William Frucht, my editor at Yale University Press, has acted as midwife for this book, encouraging, counseling, and yes, extracting.

Then of course there is one more.

THE DEMOCRATIC FAITH

Prologue

T HERE is a large literature of democratic lament. The most familiar of the lamentations is that the public is woefully uninformed about politics and public affairs. The verse that follows, as all students of public opinion know, is that ordinary citizens fall short of the coherence of thought that a democratic politics requires.

There is good reason for skepticism about whether citizens are up to the responsibilities of democratic citizenship. But an experience at the beginning of my career persuaded me that what appeared to be obviously true—that citizens were just not up to the job of democratic citizenship—was at the least not obvious and possibly not even true.

I was invited to join a large-scale research project. It offered an opportunity to work with colleagues I admired and to build and to validate measures of trust in government.

An extraordinary opportunity, but there was a problem. The deeper I got into the project, the less I understood why we were doing what we were doing. The problem ostensibly was a crisis of confidence: citizens had lost trust in government, putting the democratic enterprise at risk. In the context of the times, Vietnam was still a slaughterhouse, the process of impeaching Nixon was under way, and it seemed to me it would have been a greater problem had citizens not lost trust in government.

Unable to see how to move forward, I found myself often waking up at two or three in the morning. To get back to sleep, I developed a routine: go down to my study, pick a book, read until I felt some sense of fatigue, then truck off to bed, hopefully to sleep through the remaining hours. One night, I pulled *The Federalist Papers* off the shelf. I sat down on the sofa and began to read. After all these years, I cannot recall which Numbers I read. I do remember being suddenly struck by a question. What would I have thought if I had been reading *The Federalist Papers* when they were written? Would I have been persuaded that citizens could handle the duties of democratic citizenship? And as I asked myself the question, I knew immediately what I would have said. "A noble idea, but no way, people know too little and are too impulsive."

It is not every day that you realize that you would have made a world-class historical mistake. I would have bet against the best political idea there has ever been. Since then, I have worked to understand what it is that I failed to understand. These studies set out an answer, so far as I have come to one.

It is not an argument for optimism about the capacities of citizens. I do not believe now that they—we—are smarter or less impulsive and self-interested or more deeply informed about public affairs than I believed at the start. The key, I have become persuaded, is political institutions. We do not make our choices in a political vacuum. Citizens, at any rate a large bloc of them, can organize and simplify political choices because these choices have been organized and simplified for them by the political process itself.

That is the story I mean to tell. The starting point is the problem of preference reversals. Roughly, the problem is that the positions citizens take on an issue in one set of circumstances or at one point in time can be a poor guide to the positions they will take on in a different set of circumstances or at a different point in time. More than one problem is crowding under this tent. So there is no once-and-for-all solution. But there is an irony that has not gotten the appreciation that it deserves.

Part of the explanation of why citizens take different positions in public opinion interviews is that they are paying attention to what the interviewer is and is not saying. The metaphor of a conversation is helpful here. Conversations have a logic. We commonly count on others to comply with the rule that what they say, they say because it is relevant to the question at hand. It is an interesting irony that people can appear to vary their policy preferences for no good reason because they assume that what the interviewer has just said, she has said for a relevant reason.

It is of course one thing to be able to make coherent choices with the benefit of trustworthy information from another person. It is another thing to cope with the multitude of choices that citizens must confront. It has seemed obvious to analysts of public opinion, including me, that citizens have to make too many choices and have too little information to make them coherently. Or so I believed. But rules organize interactions with others collectively as well as individually. Citizens in turn are capable of coherence to the extent that their environment is coherent.

The particular story that I have to tell is that the choice set — the alternatives on offer — is simplified, stabilized, coordinated under the pressure of electoral competition through the medium of political parties. This radically reduces information costs: an easily acquired bit of knowledge — which is the more conservative, which the more liberal, party — provides a key to party-defined choice sets. And because the choice sets are both party-defined and ideologically labeled, large blocks of the public can organize their choices along ideological lines, notwithstanding their limited information about politics.

A lack of coherence in citizens' political thinking is not the only reason for skepticism about whether they are up to the job, though. Another is their susceptibility to intolerance.

For the longest time, all that I could see was the readiness of many to strike out against, or to condone others striking out against, those who looked different, or spoke a different language, or prayed to a different god, or came from a different background. I was not wrong in being impressed by the force of prejudice. But I have come to believe that to understand how prejudice shapes the political choices of mass publics, it is necessary to start with politics.

When I say start with politics, I mean, in the first instance, recognizing the force of political ideas and convictions. The contemporary clash over issues of race — over how much government ought to do in behalf of racial equality and how much is up to blacks themselves—is grounded in conflicting perspectives on politics. Just so far as they are liberal, Americans white and non-white alike will support government efforts to overcome racial inequality. Just so far as they are conservatives, Americans white and non-white alike will oppose liberal policies to deal with issues of race. But by the need to start with politics, I mean in the second instance that politics defines the relevance of racial prejudice to issues of race. The result, according to our studies, is ironic. Although prejudice is more common on the political right than on the left, it is politically more consequential on the political left than on the right.[1]

This seemed all that it was necessary to say until the election of the first African American president.[2] Without minimizing the numbers of white Americans who think ill of black Americans, one surely had to ask, is it possible that some politically significant number of whites think well of them? This is an idea one would like to believe is true; all the more reason to take seriously that it is false. Recognizing the limits of what can be done in a public opinion interview, that is what I attempt. Rough and ready as the analysis is, the results are not politically uninteresting. Among other things, it turns out that the magnitude of the impact of prejudice on the left has been exaggerated and that, in parallel situations, the impact of prejudice is as forceful on the right as on the left.[3]

It is not, looking back, that skepticism about a democratic politics seems to me ill founded. Indeed, in some respects, it does not go deep enough. The politically active and influential supposedly compensate for the failings of ordinary citizens.

It is true enough that studies have repeatedly shown that, compared with average citizens, political elites stand out for their stauncher commitment to democratic values. But these studies offer less comfort than has been supposed. For the lessons drawn from them depend on comparing political elites taken as a whole with the general public taken as a whole. But we do not elect the average of all political elites. We put in power Republicans or Democrats. And the cleavage between them dwarfs the difference between elites and citizens.

How, then, does my view of mass politics differ from the prevailing one? It has concentrated on cataloguing the failings of ordinary citizens—their lack of knowledge, of consistency in political ideas; of tolerance. This focus on the weaknesses of their political thinking has obscured the deep clash of coherent opposing ideologies in the electorate. The concentration on racism has kept out of sight those who think well of blacks. Above all, the insistent emphasis on the risks of mass politics has diverted attention from the greater risks of elite politics.

Or so I shall argue.

CHAPTER ONE

Preference Reversals:
A Theory of Conversational Logic

I T is a truth universally acknowledged, to follow Jane Austen's lead, that citizens do not discharge the responsibilities of democratic citizenship as they ideally should. All the same, I should like to consider the conjecture that they do a better job than has been recognized. This may seem yet another assault of hope on experience. But critiques of ordinary citizens have become so familiar—they think so little about politics, know so little about it—that it is not widely recognized just how radical they now are.

The most radical charge is this—that "most people really aren't sure what their opinions are on most political matters."[1] The charge, notice, is not that people are constitutively insincere, that they do not mean what they say when they say, for example, that government should do more to help blacks or, more likely, that blacks should do more to help themselves. It is that the preferences they express, the positions they take on issues, represent only fleeting considerations that happen to come to mind in response to a specific question, at a particular moment, in a specific set of circumstances.[2] Given only a slightly different wording of the question, or the happenstance of a slightly different *set* of circumstances, citizens might well line up on the very opposite side of the same issue.

You might call this endemic flip-flopping. I shall make use of a higher-class term, preference reversals. Preference reversals, strictly defined, are changes of preferences over exactly equivalent gambles because of logically irrelevant differences in formulation.[3] Preference reversals broadly defined are changes of preferences over substantially equivalent choices because of differences in emphasis on aspects of the alternatives on offer or accidents of what happens to be salient at a particular moment. Preference reversals conceived broadly may or may not be violations of rationality defined strictly. But, it is claimed, so many will say one thing in one set of circumstances and say the opposite in another that a fair summary is that "most people really aren't very sure what their opinions are on most political matters."[4] This claim, if valid, undercuts the presumption that citizens are up to the job of democratic citizenship. As Achen notably declared, if citizens do not know what they think about the issues of the day, "democratic theory loses its starting point."[5]

I shall examine the claim that preference reversals are endemic to the political thinking of ordinary citizens. It deserves to be examined most obviously because of its normative implications. But it deserves examination on another ground—the sheer number of different theories that have been advanced to explain it. Preference reversals have variously been attributed to citizens lacking a grounded reason to take one rather than another side of an issue; to their having a surplus of them; to the influence of top-down politics; to issue framing. I shall demonstrate that, taken individually or collectively, they do not justify a claim that preference reversals are characteristic of the political thinking of citizens about issues at the center of contemporary American politics.

My objective, though, is constructive, not critical. It would be irrational if citizens' choices were invariant regardless of circumstance. The question is thus the extent to which, as Bartels well puts it, preferences depend on "*arbitrary* features of the context, formulation or procedure used to elicit those preferences."[6] My aim, therefore, is to show that changes in policy positions apparently made for no good reason often turn out to be changes for a relevant reason. But first I want to call attention to the best reason to believe that what I think is true, is false.

THE TOP-OF-THE-HEAD MODEL
OF POLITICAL THINKING

Converse, in his classic essay on mass belief systems, suggested that when citizens have not given thought to an issue, and therefore have no good reason to take one or the other side of the issue, they choose a side as though at random to conceal their having failed to give the issue thought.[7] Zaller and Feldman turned Converse's conjecture upside down. The problem, they contended, is not that citizens lack a genuine reason to prefer one policy alternative to another. The problem is just the opposite. They have too many reasons, some favoring one side of an issue, others the opposite side. Whether they take one or the other side of an issue depends on the happenstance that more reasons favoring or opposing a policy come to mind. Hence Zaller and Feldman's baptism of their theory as a "top-of-the-head" model of political thinking.[8]

Theirs has become the leading theory of politics and public opinion for a battery of reasons—the scope and diversity of phenomena for which their theory gives a credible account, the originality of their empirical analysis, and the sheer verve of their presentation—their argument is developed in the form of axioms followed by deductions (or predictions) derived from the axioms. What have been missing, however, are direct tests of its validity. As Bartels has observed, "Most citations . . . seem to have appealed to Zaller as evidence rather than subjecting his work to the sort of intense critical scrutiny that is so often taken to be the hallmark of the scientific process."[9] I therefore propose to do just that.

The intuition underpinning the top-of-the-head model is this: Asked whether they favor or oppose more government help for blacks, for example, people first call to mind reasons why they might take one rather than the other side. Depending on the balance of considerations pro and con that happens to come to mind on any particular occasion, they take a position in favor of or opposed to government help for blacks.[10] I must admit that I don't find this intuition particularly plausible on many issues. It seems more likely to me that, rather than first sitting through a roll call of salient considerations why they should or should not support, say, affirmative action, most Americans, black and white, have their positions down on race and abortion and so on.[11] But if I and some others have trouble with the intuition underpinning the top-of-the-head model, there is no shortage of experts who find it not only plausible but nearly self-evidently right.

This intuition—first canvass one's thoughts, then take a position—provides a foundational premise of the Zaller-Feldman model, or as they put it, the Ambivalence Axiom:

> Most people possess opposing considerations on most issues, that is, considerations that might lead them to decide the issue either way.[12]

Note that "opposing" is used here in a special sense. Ordinarily, ambivalence refers to a state of being "*simultaneously* pulled in opposing directions."[13] I put "simultaneously" in italics because the customary purpose of the concept of ambivalence is to pick out a state of psychological conflict. There are two points here, connected but distinguishable. The first is that ambivalence, in the Zaller-Feldman conception, rather than involving simultaneously opposing beliefs and emotions, can and frequently does refer to a circumstance when a consideration favoring a political choice comes to mind on one occasion, but a consideration opposing it comes to mind on another.[14]

The second point is that ambivalence standardly refers to a state of tension and discomfort. Just so far as one is ambivalent, one is being pulled in opposing directions. To be simultaneously pulled in opposing directions is not pleasant. Hence the need to resolve dissonance. For Zaller and Feldman, however, "the heart of our argument is that for most people, most of the time, there is no need to reconcile or even to recognize their contradictory reactions to events and issues."[15] That citizens are unaware of contradictory beliefs and feelings is the heart of their argument because, if people were aware of them, they would strive for consistency to relieve the discomfort of their clashing ideas and feelings. To maintain a stock of conflicting considerations without feeling a need to reduce the conflict among them, it is necessary that people can be ambivalent without feeling a need to resolve the ambivalence.

Reconceiving a concept is not a fault. On the contrary, it can be a route to original discoveries. For Zaller and Feldman, the point of the concept of ambivalence is to bring out the process by which citizens almost literally construct their position on a policy—"by averaging across the range of competing ideas . . . that happen to be salient at the moment of response."[16] And how is the salience of competing ideas determined? By "a stochastic sampling process, where considerations that have been recently thought are somewhat more likely to be sampled."[17]

Only one more detail needs to be nailed down. According to Zaller and Feldman, "most people are internally conflicted over most political issues."[18] Zaller, in his follow-up analysis, repeats this: "most people, on most issues."[19] I think it is a mistake to take these words literally. It is not necessary that opposing considerations be precisely equal in number, nor that a numerical majority of the public be of two minds on the largest number of issues. Still, the more modest the fraction of the public that is of two minds, and the more modest the number of issues that they are of two minds about, the more modest the validity of the top-of-the-head model.

The question then is, what portion of the public is ambivalent as defined by Zaller and Feldman? To answer this question, I am going to reanalyze the same data that they analyzed. But first a cautionary warning is in order. It is not well understood, notwithstanding Zaller and Feldman's clarity on the point, that their empirical analysis is based on one small-scale, two-wave pilot study (N = 437 and 360, respectively). This effort is entirely suited to opening the door to a new line of inquiry, though it is not nearly enough to close it. This cautionary warning, need I say, applies as much to my reanalysis as to their original analysis.

Warning given, how do Zaller and Feldman operationally measure ambivalence? Their objective is to develop a theory of how people respond to questions in public opinion interviews. But they cannot do that by asking questions the way they are asked in public opinion interviews. It is not self-evident that the right strategy to develop a theory to account for how people answer questions in public opinion interviews is to explain how they answer questions asked in a different way than they usually are asked in public opinion interviews. But to bring into view what they believe to be the heart of the matter, they must turn to two unusual procedures. In the first, respondents are asked to choose between two opposing policies. Their answer is recorded, but before asking the next question, the interviewer says, "thinking about the question you just answered, I'd like you to tell me what ideas came to mind as you were answering the question. Exactly what things went through your mind?" This they dub the Retrospective probe.

The second technique is quite different. Respondents are asked the same questions, but the interviewer stops them before they can answer, and says, "Before telling me how you feel about this, could you tell me what kinds of things come to mind when you think . . . about the first policy?" (Any others?) Then, having recorded verbatim the responses to the first policy alternative, the interviewer asks the respondents what kinds of things came to mind when they thought about the opposing alternative.[20] This second technique they dub the Stop-and-Think probe.

One last detail: in addition to the "conflicting considerations" measure of ambivalence, they present two other measures. I am not sure why they do this. Only the measure of "conflicting considerations" bears on their theory, while the other two measures of ambivalence do not appear in the subsequent analyses.[21] To provide a complete picture, Table 1.1 presents a replication of their original results for all measures of ambivalence, irrelevant as well as relevant.[22]

Consider the two measures that appear once. Both show ambivalence is the exception. The median percentage of respondents completely free of ambivalence is 80 percent in the Retrospective condition and 71 percent in the Stop-and-Think condition. The case for the Zaller-Feldman theory of ambivalence as "conflicting considerations" rests, as it should, on the pervasiveness of conflicting considerations.[23]

How commonplace is ambivalence defined as "conflicting considerations"? The answer, Table 1.1 shows, depends almost entirely on the method of measurement. The Retrospective technique turns up evidence of minimal ambivalence: the median number without ambivalence, in any degree whatever, is 73 percent. The Stop-and-Think technique, however, turns up evidence of massive ambivalence: the median number with at least some degree of ambivalence is 68 percent.

It is a bit unsettling that whether many people or only a

Table 1.1 A replication of Zaller-Feldman measures
of ambivalence on political issues

Conflicts	Retrospective			Stop and think		
	Jobs	Services	Blacks	Jobs	Services	Blacks
0	79	61	77	37	32	30
1	18	30	19	28	29	22
2	4	5	3	22	21	24
3+	0	4	0	13	18	24
Ambivalence						
0	77	83	79	63	72	71
1+	23	17	21	37	28	29
Two-sided						
0	86	94	81	73	93	72
1+	14	6	19	27	7	28
Sample size	108	109	118	173	168	165

Source: Zaller and Feldman 1992, p. 591.

few are ambivalent hinges on using one measurement technique and ignoring the other. More unsettling still, there are good grounds to wonder what the more unusual technique, the Stop-and-Think probe, actually measures. Respondents are expressly asked to report what things come to mind, first if they stop to consider one side of an issue, then next, if they consider the other side, what things come to mind.[24] Lodge and Taber, citing an array of studies in addition to their own results, observe that "asking people 'to stop and think,' to ruminate before responding . . . will bring *less*-important cognitive considerations to mind and thereupon deflect the evaluation off its online trajectory."[25] One might reply that, even so, there will only be evidence of ambivalence if people are in fact ambivalent. But it is not obvious that it is ambivalence that the Stop-and-Think probe measures. It calls to mind measures of integrative complexity—that is, a readiness to distinguish among and then to integrate competing considerations, an interpretation, it is worth noting, that goes hand in hand with Zaller and Feldman's finding of a positive association between political awareness and the volume of considerations mentioned.[26]

Enough questions and concerns, you must be thinking—but there is one more difficulty, and I will pay close attention to it, both because it is the most worrisome and because it has gone unnoticed. The Zaller-Feldman measure of the number of conflicting considerations that a person possesses is "a count of the number of opposing remarks by each person that can be paired against another. If, for example, a respondent makes two comments with a liberal thrust and two with a conservative thrust, his score on the conflict scale is two. If he makes three (or more) on one side of the issue and only two on the other, the conflict score is still two, since the number of opposing comments that can be paired remains two."[27]

What, exactly, does this "Pairing" rule entail? Consider two people, Albert and Barbara. Albert thinks of two reasons to support government assistance for blacks and two reasons to oppose it. Barbara, like Albert, mentions two reasons to support government help for blacks; however, unlike Albert, she points to ten reasons to oppose it. According to the Pairing rule, Albert and Barbara are equally ambivalent. Both receive a score of 2. This cannot be right. They are not equally or approximately or even roughly alike. Albert has the same number of reasons to oppose government help for blacks as to support it. Barbara has five times as many reasons to oppose it as to support it.[28]

How many more reasons to take one side of the issue than the other must a person have to have a definite view of the matter? If I have *at least twice as many* reasons to take one side of an issue than the other, and each reason has the same weight as any other; and if I decide, as Zaller and Feldman propose, by averaging the reasons pro and con, then I'm not in doubt which side of the issue to take. However, to bring out the consequences of the pairing rule, I have also calculated the percentages classified as equally conflicted that have *at least three times as many* thoughts on one side than on the other; *at least four times as many* thoughts on one side than on the other; and *at least five times as many* thoughts on one side as on the other.

To determine the number of false positives—that is, respondents classified as equally conflicted who in fact have one-sided views—I reanalyzed the Zaller-Feldman data. The left-hand panel of Table 1.2 reports the percentages of false positives for the retrospective technique; the right-hand panel, the percentages for the Stop-and-Think technique. The results in the Stop-and-Think condition have been put in italics, since it provided the strongest evidence for the Zaller-Feldman top-of-the-head model of political thinking.

How many of those classified as having conflicting considerations actually have one-sided views? Take the standard of having a one-sided view as calling to mind at least twice as many reasons to take one side of an issue than another. For

Table 1.2 False positives: Percentage of respondents classified as having an equal number of conflicting considerations with substantially more thoughts on one side

Actually unconflicted definition	Retrospective			Stop and Think		
	Aid blacks	Provide jobs	Provide more services	Aid blacks	Provide jobs	Provide more services
At least 2× as many thoughts on one side as the other (exactly 2 on one side and 1 on the other excluded)	33.3	44	43	62	52	61
At least 3× as many thoughts on one side as the other	29	44	4.5	33	33	5
At least 4× as many thoughts on one side as the other	15	17	29	33	22	32
At least 5× as many thoughts on one side as the other	15	9	14	25	12	223

the sake of fairness, I treat the special case of those with two reasons on one side and one on the other as too close to call and therefore count it in favor of Zaller and Feldman.

Table 1.2 shows that most of those classified as equally conflicted according to the Pairing rule are false positives. Thus, 61.7 percent on aid to blacks, 52.3 percent on government providing jobs, and 61.4 percent on more services have *at least twice* as many reasons in mind to take one rather than the other side of the issue. Now, consider an extreme standard for false positives. According to the Pairing rule, one out of every three classified as equally conflicted has *at least four* times as many thoughts on side than the other. I do not see how to justify the Pairing rule.

The top-of-the-head model is advanced as a general theory of the survey responses to political issues, with the emphasis on general. Its up-or-down claim is that "many citizens are equally inconsistent in their reactions to different aspects of the same issue."[29] The data do not show this. I would suggest that to believe that most white Americans are of two minds about issues of race or welfare or immigration—that is, the issues at the core of American politics—misses how deep political cleavages go in contemporary American politics.

NON-ATTITUDES AND TOP-DOWN POLITICS

A second, more recent line of research approaches the analysis of preference reversals and asks to what extent citizens follow the lead of political elites. I shall apply the label "top-down politics" to this line of research.

It is long and well established that party supporters respond to party cues. They are, for example, more likely to support candidates of their party and policy positions of their party if they bear their party's labels.[30] However, to observe party supporters following the lead of leaders of their party is not, in and of itself, evidence of responding to "*arbitrary* features of the context, formulation or procedure of a political choice."[31]

If the leaders of a party take a stand on an issue in the course of a campaign, and supporters of their party pick it up, it is descriptively accurate to say that the supporters are learning and adopting the positions of their party. Normatively, learning has positive overtones. It points to the possibility that voters are paying attention to politics, taking in new information, and updating their preferences. But there is, of course, another, less happy possibility. They may be following their party's leaders blindly, reflexively. If so, though their responsiveness may not be strictly arbitrary, it may nonetheless be further evidence for the claim that citizens readily change positions mindlessly.

It would be entirely understandable to take the view that this is a specimen example of a question you would love to know the answer to, but which, if you truly know what it will take to answer it, you would appreciate an answer is out of reach. Three requirements must be met: (1) knowing positions of voters, if any, before an issue becomes salient, (2) learning the positions of party leaders when it becomes salient, and (3) knowing the positions of the *same* voters after it becomes salient. The second condition, in isolation from the first and third, is trivially easy to meet; the second, in conjunction with the first, is harder, but not all that hard. Satisfying all three simultaneously is extraordinarily difficult.

In a pathbreaking study, Lenz has met this challenge, analyzing reactions to the issues of European integration in the 1997 British election, Social Security in the 2000 U.S. presidential election, public works jobs in the 1976 U.S. presidential election, and defense spending in the 1980 U.S. presidential election.[32] In all four elections, an issue that was not salient before the campaign began became not merely salient but central to the election over the course of the campaign. In addition, the positions of opposing candidates and parties on the issue were well publicized. And, critically, the same individuals were interviewed before the campaign began and after it ended. Therefore, Lenz was able to determine not merely whether voters changed their positions but who among them was most and least likely to do so.

His results show that a large segment of the electorate, on the order of between 30 and 40 percent depending on the issue, learned the position of their party over the course of the election campaign. As important, he also shows that "learners are not changing their votes to reflect their issue opinions . . . they are changing their issue opinions to reflect their votes."[33] His conclusion: "Campaign and media attention to an issue led individuals to learn the issue positions of the candidates or parties and then to adopt the position of their preferred party or candidate as their own."[34] Voters are learning, but what they are learning is not a basis for voting. It is the other way around. They adopt the position of the party or candidate that they already prefer and for whom they will in any case vote.

As Lenz puts it, "The learners are not changing their votes to reflect their issue opinions, that is, not exhibiting learning effects. Instead, they are changing their issue opinions to reflect their votes."[35]

Lenz's work is a major advance. It makes a compelling case that voters can learn during a campaign—learn in the sense of picking out and picking up the position of the party or candidate they prefer. But what does this signify? In Lenz's view, no more than that voters are capable of following the leader. Perhaps this is the right characterization. But it is not necessarily the right one.

Consider the kind of issues that are being analyzed. All were nonissues before the campaign. All then burst into prominence suddenly, unexpectedly. It is no accident that this is so. For Lenz, a requirement was that the issues voters focused on during an election campaign were not issues that they were paying attention to before the campaign. Not surprisingly, then, most of the voters did not know parties' positions on the issues before the election.[36]

The focus, then, is on a class of issues unlike those that the political parties have built their reputations contesting— for example, on the extent to which government should help those who are poorly off rather than people taking responsibility for dealing with their own problems. It should not be surprising that party supporters would look to their party for guidance when an issue they had no reason to think through suddenly and unexpectedly becomes prominent in a campaign. Moreover, in determining their vote, their views on this issue were of little consequence. If voters make the same decisions in the voting booth that they would have made if one of these meteor issues had not flashed into sight, in what sense then can it be said that partisans are robotically following a political leader?[37]

The question is not whether parties can serve as reference groups for their supporters.[38] It is whether, by using a political party as a reference group, supporters of a party are blindly following its lead. Two issues need to be addressed. The first is the weight that voters attach to policy information. The answer, previous research suggests, is precious little.[39] But in one of those intellectual moves that look obvious only after the fact, Bullock has transformed the terms of argument.[40] Reviewing previous research, he flags a design feature that had gone unremarked. In past studies of the relative influence of partisan cues and policy information, he points out, the information provided about policies is brief and vague—often no more than a sentence or two. How, Bullock asks, would partisans react if they received an amount of information akin to what they get in a real-life newspaper article—say, more than in a low- but less than in a high-circulation newspaper? Carrying out a sequence of large-scale experiments, he shows that partisan cues matter—it would be a mark against his results if they did not correspond at all to those of previous studies—but that policy considerations, if presented in substantive detail, matter more. His conclusion: "People rarely possess even a modicum of information about policies; but when they do, their attitudes seem to be affected at least as much by that information as by cues from party elites."[41]

The implication of Lenz's argument is that party supporters, by virtue of their attachment to their party, follow their party's lead reflexively. That surely is right for some partisans and, what is more, right for more of them for some issues. Bullock's analysis, however, calls to mind the possibility that whether partisans follow the lead of their party may depend on what they know.

The research of Slothuus and colleagues has broken new ground by examining the reactions of partisans when their party reverses a position. Slothuus exploits the Social Democratic Party's reversal of its position on early retirement during the 2005 Danish national election season. His results show that only supporters of the Social Democratic Party reversed their position from favoring early retirement to opposing it. On its face, this is seemingly a prototypical example of following the leader. Seemingly, I say, because they adopt the new position of their party if, but only if, it is consistent with their general view that the welfare state is under economic stress.[42]

Building on this result, Leeper and Slothuus bring out the interplay between elite cues and general predispositions in opinion formation. They presciently identified in advance an issue, whether Denmark should or should not join the European Unified Patent Court, that was barely visible to the public before the coming election but that would become salient during the election. They designed a novel multi-wave panel, incorporating randomized experiments, to assess reactions at different points in the campaign to the issue of Denmark joining the European Unified Patent Court.

Their design allows us to distinguish two mechanisms of elite influence. One mechanism is yielding; the other is understanding. Both entail complying with a cue, but one entails a reflexive response to a party label, the other getting the point of policy arguments.[43] Leeper and Slothuus find evidence of yielding, particularly among those without a general attitude pro or con toward European integration and understanding, most clearly among those whose general orientation toward European integration fits with their party's new position.

Leeper and Slothuus exploit a rare event, a party reversing its position, through an innovative design—a repeat interview with respondents randomly selected at different time points in a campaign. Boudreau reports results reinforcing the importance of distinguishing understanding from yielding, grounded on a randomized experiment. Capitalizing on an imaginative design, Boudreau investigates the independent and interdependent impacts of party cues and policy considerations. Her results show that party supporters balk at following their party when its position is at odds with their values—provided (and this is a proviso to underline) the alternative policy is not identified with the opposing party.[44]

All in all, this body of research points to the possibility that partisans may respond to cues in light of the political beliefs they hold—a possibility worth exploring more deeply.

RELEVANT REASONS AND THE CONTINGENCY OF CHOICE

The Claim of Issue Framing and Choice

The concept of issue framing grew out of a deeply original line of thought in the analysis of media discourse and public opinion.[45] Media discourse, Gamson and Modigliani proposed, consists of interpretive packages, each with an internal structure, each giving meaning to an issue or event in the public domain. At the center of each package, they asserted, "is a central organizing idea, or frame."[46] A frame, by incorporating and condensing a set of "metaphors, catchphrases, visual images, moral appeals, and other symbolic devices," supplies a readily comprehensible basis suggesting both how to think about the issue at hand and how to justify what should be done about it.[47] Frames are not reducible simply to an argument on one or another side of an issue. They are broader, as Nelson and Kinder observe, making salient "how it should be thought about, and may go so far as to recommend what (if anything) should be done."[48]

Consider Nelson, Clawson, and Oxley's classic study of issue framing and support for civil liberties. Creating videotapes mimicking local television newscasts, Nelson, Clawson, and Oxley presented respondents in one experimental condition with a story highlighting the value of free speech, and respondents in a second condition with a story highlighting the risk of violence and disorder. Comparing the two experimental conditions, they found significantly more support for the right of the KKK to hold a rally when the issue was framed in terms of freedom than when it was framed in terms of the risk of violence. The results of the Public Rally experiment thus dramatize the subversiveness of preference reversals. Framed one way, public support for freedom of speech is strong; framed another way, weak.[49]

It does not pay to underestimate guessing, fuzzy thinking, choices made on the fly, dressing up one's views on political issues to present a more favorable impression, and other petty pathologies of public opinion. Nothing I say should be taken to minimize, still less to deny, the fact that people are perfectly capable of making a hash of political choices. But there is, I believe, another way of looking at the results of framing experiments. It is that citizens may have relevant reasons presented to them on particular occasions for supporting one of the alternatives on offer that they otherwise would have opposed and vice versa.

The Concept of a Relevant Reason

Reason is the operative term. A reason, as I shall use the term, is a belief or goal that justifies a choice. But what qualifies as a justification?

Three conditions must be met. The first is substantive relevance. To count as a reason, the belief or goal must carry water. It must, that is to say, be objectively *relevant* to the choice at hand. By objective relevance, I mean that a reason would be judged by an impartial observer as a justification for preferring one of the alternatives on offer to the others.

Substantive relevance is a necessary but not a sufficient condition. Just because an impartial judge would count a consideration as substantively relevant, it does not follow that particular individuals would—or should—consider it relevant.[50] Precisely the point about many political choices is that what counts as a justification is in dispute. Accordingly, to count as a relevant reason to favor one alternative over another, a justification must be subjectively as well as objectively relevant—that is, it must resonate in light of the beliefs and goals of the person making the choice. A citizen who is concerned about law and order will—and should—be disposed to give more weight to threats to law and order than to freedom of expression. Conversely, a citizen who is more concerned about freedom of expression than to securing public safety will—and should—be disposed to give more weight to threats to First Amendment rights than to threats to public safety. Both are making a choice for good reason—good, that is, in light of their views of the matter.

The third condition is conversational relevance. Conversations, Grice posits, are cooperative efforts. Participants, on this view, contribute to a conversation in order to achieve the goal of the exchange in which they are engaged.[51] From this premise of cooperative effort, Grice deduces a number of regulative maxims. The two most important for our purposes are the Maxim of Quality and the Maxim of Relevance. The Maxim of Quality stipulates that a participant in a conversation may count on other participants complying with the rule "Do not say what you believe to be false." The Maxim of Relevance stipulates that a participant in a conversation may also count on other participants complying with the rule "Make your conversational contribution relevant to the purpose of the conversation."[52] Together, the Maxims of Quality and Relevance cash out in an injunction. If I give you a justification for choosing one alternative over another, you will know I did so because I believe it is consistent with both my beliefs and goals and yours.

Objective, subjective, and conversational relevance, then, are three conditions of reasons qualifying as relevant reasons for choosing one alternative over others. I acknowledge that to talk of citizens making political choices for a relevant reason is not common practice. But to do so is less of a departure from common practice than it may seem to be. It provides a way of understanding just why people do and should take account of the immediate circumstances when making a choice. People have reasons for taking account of considerations presented to them to favor one alternative over the others on offer, and what is more, they do so in light of their beliefs and goals.

Reasons About Reasons: Framing Experiments

In their classic experiment, Nelson, Oxley, and Clawson showed that the readiness of citizens to support or to oppose the right of an extreme group to hold a public rally depends on how the issue is framed.[53] They interpreted their results as evidence of the malleability of political preferences—a plausible interpretation but not the only one conceivable. To bring out an alternative, Theriault and I replicated their study with a nationally representative sample. In one condition, respondents were asked whether a group with very extreme views should be allowed to hold a public rally "given the risk of violence"; in another condition, whether the group should be allowed to hold a public rally "given the importance of free speech."[54] The results of the replication fully support Nelson, Oxley, and Clawson's finding of a framing effect. When the issue of freedom of assembly is framed in terms of free speech, 83 percent support the group's right to hold a rally. In contrast, when it is framed in terms of risk of violence, support is cut in half: now, only a minority—a sizable minority, 41 percent, but a minority nonetheless—stand by freedom of assembly. On its face, this is compelling evidence of the kind of preference reversals that vitiate a presupposition that citizens can make coherent and consistent choices. A majority takes one side when an issue is framed one way, the opposite side when it is framed another way.

Preference reversals are changes in position made for ar-

Table 1.3 Two frames: The public rally experiment

	Risk of violence	Importance of free speech
Order much more important than freedom	.34 (.05)	.64 (.04)
Order somewhat more important than freedom	.33 (.03)	.67 (.03)
Freedom somewhat more important than order	.47 (.05)	.76 (.03)
Freedom much more important than order	.55 (.07)	.78 (.05)

Source: Sniderman and Theriault 2004.

bitrary reasons. Take account of the conditions of relevance, however, and it becomes clear that the results of the public rally experiment are evidence of changes made for a relevant not an arbitrary reason. Table 1.3 shows the levels of support for allowing the group to hold a public rally conditional on both the way the issue was framed for individuals and the relative priority that they give to order and freedom.

Manifestly, the two frames—the principle of free speech and the risk of violence—are substantively relevant to a decision about whether the group should be allowed to hold a public rally. So, too, are people's goals and values as justifications pro and con. Accordingly, as part of our study of framing, we assessed the relative importance of two values that sometimes come into conflict. Specifically, respondents were asked: "If you had to choose between guaranteeing law and order in society or guaranteeing individual freedom, which would you say is more important?" Having picked one of the two as the more important, they were asked how much more important it is. A four-category index was then constructed, gathering together those who rank order as much more important than freedom, order as somewhat or a little more important than freedom, freedom as somewhat or a little more important than order, and finally, freedom as much more important than order.

Following the template of the standard framing experiment, Table 1.3 shows the level of support for the group's right to hold a public rally depending on whether respondents were assigned to the risk of violence or the importance of free speech frame and the degree of their commitment to values of order and individual freedom, if forced to choose between them. Responses are scored from 0 to 1. The higher the score, the more support for the extreme group's right to hold a public rally.

Consider the seemingly contradictory responses in the two experimental conditions. Those who rank order as much more important than freedom flip-flop. In the risk of violence condition, they plainly oppose the group's right to hold a public rally (X = .34, s.e .05). In the importance of free speech condition, they just as strongly support it (X = .64, s.e. .04). The flip-flop of those who rank freedom as much more important than order is nearly as striking. In the importance of free speech condition, they overwhelmingly support the group's right to hold a public rally. In the risk of violence condition, only a bare majority of them (X = .55, s.e. .07) do. The results would seem to provide even stronger support for the irrationality of preference reversals. Depending on how choices are framed, citizens are likely not merely to respond differently in one frame than another, but also to choose the alternative at odds with their general view of the matter.

That is one way to read the results. Suppose, however, that you are participating in the public rally experiment. Naturally, you will have given some thought to what matters in life—your own and that of the larger society. Asked which is more important to you, you reply that "guaranteeing individual freedom" is much more important than "guaranteeing law and order." You accordingly will and should be predisposed to support the group's right to hold a public rally, other things equal. But other things are not equal if you have been assigned to the risk of violence condition. The interviewer says to you:

> This next question is about a group that has very extreme political views. Suppose they wanted to hold a public rally to express their views. Given the risk of violence, would you be in favor of or opposed to allowing this group to hold a rally?

The Maxim of Quality stipulates that a participant in a conversation may count on fellow participants complying with the rule "Do not say what you believe to be false." Adhering to the Maxim of Quality, the interviewer would not say what she believed to be false. Accordingly, when she says, "Given the risk of violence . . . ," you will and should draw the inference that there is in fact a risk of violence. In addition, the Maxim of Relevance stipulates that a participant in a conversation may also count on other participants complying with the rule "Make your conversational contribution relevant to the purpose of the conversation." You accordingly will and should draw the inference that, in deciding whether a rally should be allowed, you should take into account the risk of violence.

How, then, should we decide if your decision is reason-based? Yes, you rank preserving individual freedom as more important than guaranteeing law and order. But because you believe that individual freedom is more important, even much more important, it does not follow that you believe that public safety is unimportant. On the contrary, you surely believe that ensuring public safety is important, and depending on circumstances, the most important consideration. Having been informed of a risk of violence, given the Maxims of Quality and Relevance, you have a conversationally relevant reason to believe that you should take account of the risk of violence in this particular circumstance. Grounding your choice on risk of violence leads you to make a different choice than you ordinarily would make. But it is a different choice because you are taking account of immediately relevant facts. And, in taking account of them, you are not sidetracking your commitment to freedom of expression, for you are still markedly more likely to support the group's right to hold a rally than a person who believes that order is much more important than individual freedom (X = .55, s.e. .07, compared with .34, s.e. .05).

The same line of reasoning applies to those who rank guaranteeing law and order as much more important than guaranteeing individual freedom. Someone warned "Given the risk of violence . . ." would and should weight more heavily the prudence of canceling the rally. But by ranking public safety as more important than individual freedom, it does not follow that the speaker believes that freedom is unimportant. When attention is specifically directed to the value of free speech, following the Maxims of Quality and Relevance, people will and should treat this as a reason to support the right of assembly. In doing so, they are not "flip-flopping." They are taking into account a relevant reason, singled out for attention by the person that they are talking politics with.

There are two takeaway lessons from these results, I believe. First, values anchor citizens even when, by virtue of taking account of immediate circumstances, they take a different position than they otherwise would. Second, framing experiments, far from being proof of respondents making a choice for no good reason, often are instances of making a choice for a relevant reason—relevant substantively, subjectively, and conversationally—to favor one of the alternatives on offer over the others.

Reasons vs. Pseudo-Reasons

The results from the public rally experiment support a claim that citizens make choices consistent with a relevant reason at hand to choose one alternative over another. But it does not follow that, because citizens make choices for good reasons, they do not also make choices for no good reason. By making a choice for no good reason, I mean making a choice for what superficially appears to be a reason but in fact has only the form, but not the substance, of a reason.

Consider a classic experiment designed to demonstrate "the mindlessness of ostensibly thoughtful action."[55] Subjects line up to use a Xerox machine. A secret confederate of the experiment jumps the queue, saying, "Excuse me. I have to make a copy." This has the logical form of reason. But it is vacuous. It has no substance. It is a pseudo-reason. Everyone in line is waiting to make a copy. Yielding to a pseudo-reason may outwardly appear mindful. It actually is mindless.

The Xerox experiment suggests a way to probe preference reversals. First, just as in a standard public opinion interview, ask respondents their position on an issue. Then, when they have taken a position, attempt to change it by presenting a counterargument. Here is where the idea of pseudo-reason comes into play. In one experimental condition, respondents were presented with a relevant argument to reconsider their position.[56] In the other experimental condition, they were presented with an argument that had the form, not the substance, of a reason to reconsider their position. Specifically, if respondents took the position that unemployment benefits should be increased, half the time they received a content-laden counterargument: "If unemployment benefits are too high, the unemployed will not be encouraged to look for a job." The other half of the time, they were given a content-free reason: "However, if one thinks of all the problems this will create. . . ." Alternatively, if respondents took the position that unemployment benefits should not be increased, a parallel process occurred. Half the time, they were told: "However, with today's benefits, there are many families who cannot get by." The other half of the time, they were told: "However, if one thinks of all the problems this will create. . . ."[57] In all conditions, after hearing a counterargument, all were asked whether they would change their mind as to whether unemployment benefits should be increased or not.

Who is most likely to detect the difference between genuine and bogus counterarguments? It is reasonable to suppose that the more knowledgeable people are about politics, the more adept they will be at spotting the difference between a relevant reason and a pseudo-reason. The vertical axis in the left panel of Figure 1.1 shows the probability of change in response to a counterargument and level of political sophistication: the higher the line, the greater the probability of change. The horizontal axis tracks level of political information: the further to the right, the more knowledgeable about politics. The left panel focuses on respondents presented with a content-free counterargument.

If the common sense prediction is right and political sophistication and gullibility are negatively related, the curve will slope sharply down from left to right. Instead, strikingly, the response curve is flat. The less sophisticated are as good as the more sophisticated at spotting a bogus counterargument. This result is a surprise; certainly it was to me. It is only one piece of evidence. But the capacity of the less sophisticated to be as adept at spotting a vacuous counterargument is a caution against exaggerating the mindlessness of citizens, including the less politically informed and sophisticated.

Naturally enough, the more politically knowledgeable citizens are, the more likely the positions that they take on specific issues are to be consistent with their overall outlook on politics. All the same, choosing a policy position is a probabilistic process. Two outcomes therefore need to be distinguished, one more common than the other. The more

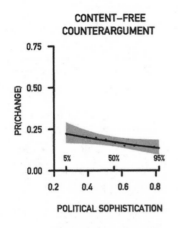

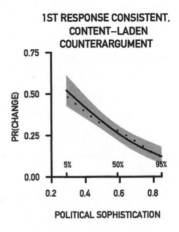

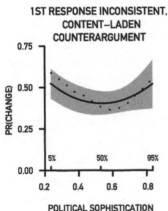

Figure 1.1. Mapping from political sophistication to probability of change, by status of initial response and type of counterargument

common outcome is that the less politically sophisticated, by virtue of being less politically sophisticated, choose a position on an issue unaware that it is at odds with the overall outlook on politics that they nominally profess. The less common outcome is that the more politically sophisticated, notwithstanding being more politically sophisticated, make a misstep and choose a position at odds with their overall view of the matter. How should we think about how a more politically sophisticated citizen and a less politically sophisticated citizen respond to a content-laden counterargument when the initial position that they have taken on a specific issue is out of line with their overall outlook on politics?

One can change one's mind for two quite different reasons: because of the persuasive force of a content-laden counterargument or the force of counterargumentation itself. The difference between the two corresponds to the distinction between understanding and yielding. The outcome, it is worth underlining, is the same either way: a change of position. But it is the same outcome for quite different reasons. Yielding is changing one's position without having a substantively relevant reason for doing so. Understanding is changing one's position because one has a substantively relevant reason to do so. A connection to political sophistication and yielding is obvious. Those with little information to buttress their opinions are the most likely to yield to a content-laden counterargument. And understanding? So far as the force of an argument made to liberals depends on their appreciation that they should find it persuasive by virtue of being liberals, then the force of the argument will vary positively with their level of political sophistication. The more politically knowledgeable and aware, the more likely they will be to find the argument persuasive. Ditto for conservatives.

The middle panel of Figure 1.1 shows the probability of change for those whose initial position is consistent with their overall ideological orientation, again conditional on their level of political sophistication. Resistance to content counterarguments is lowest for the least sophisticated, highest for the most sophisticated. The change curve falls sharply from left to right. The probability of change, in response to a content counterargument, approaches 50 percent among the least sophisticated, then plunges sharply with increases in sophistication, bottoming out at 5 percent among the most sophisticated.

The bottom panel of Figure 1.1 shows how respondents whose initial position is at odds with their overall ideological orientation react in response to a content counterargument. Again, they are arrayed on the horizontal axis, from least to most politically sophisticated. The "error correction" hypothesis leads to a prediction that the likelihood of change is highest for the most sophisticated: by virtue of being politically sophisticated, they are more likely to spot that their initial response is at odds with their ideological outlook. The "yielding" hypothesis leads to a prediction that it is highest for the least sophisticated: by virtue of being less sophisticated, they are more likely to find a content counterargument persuasive. If both hypotheses are upheld, the relationship between probability of change and level of political sophistication will be highest at the extremes, lowest in the middle—which is just what the bottom panel of Figure 1.1 shows. The probability of change curve is curvilinear: highest among the least and most politically sophisticated, lowest among those in the middle. It follows that two forms of information processing tied to political sophistication should be distinguished: the less politically aware and sophisticated yield to cues because they lack the informational resources to resist; the more politically sophisticated, because they have the informational resources to understand the point.

TAKEAWAY

It is understandably a common practice, when two opposing hypotheses are put to the test and only one meets it, to conclude that the hypothesis that survived the test is right and the one that failed it is wrong. I suspect all the same that it should be an uncommon practice. There are fewer hypotheses that, fully specified, are truly mutually exclusive than is usually supposed. But whatever it is sensible to do as matter of common practice, it does not make sense to conclude that, if the evidence at hand is consistent with the account of contingent reasons that I have set out and inconsistent with the top-of-the-head model, that the former is right, the latter wrong. The question to ask is, under what conditions does one do a better job, and under what conditions does the other do the better job?

It would be a mistake to read this as a plea for amity. It is an argument for clarity. If I call to mind the thousands of interviews that I have listened to in studies of race and politics over the years, the sense that white Americans were ambivalent or uncertain what they thought or felt about affirmative action or welfare or government programs in general to help black Americans is not what comes to mind. They knew what they thought, knew how they felt. The same, if not to quite the same degree, applies to the studies that my colleagues and I have done on attitudes toward gay rights at the height of the AIDS crisis, concerns over multiculturalism in the Netherlands just after the assassination of Pim Fortuyn, and the insistence that individuals and groups who are struggling with problems take responsibility for tackling and overcoming them, among others.

This is not a random sample of political issues. These issues are at the center of controversy. I believe the premise that voters have genuine attitudes about them does a better job of accounting for their reactions than the opposing premise that they construct their position on the spot, as it were. Hence the double objective of this chapter: first the negative one, to critically examine the strongest evidence in support of the top-of-the-head model, then the positive one, to show that choices that citizens are making for seemingly no good reason often are being made for a relevant reason.[58]

I do not doubt that there are issues for which the top-of-the-head model of thinking does the better job. Nor do I doubt that, even for some issues at the center of the contest for political power, it does a better job for a portion of the public. This may sound like an anodyne qualification. It is anything but. As I mean to demonstrate next, the failure to develop a political theory of the heterogeneity of the electorate has obscured one of its pivotal features in contemporary politics — the emergence of a large bloc of citizens who engage politics on an ideological basis.

CHAPTER TWO

An Ecological Theory
of Ideological Consistency

Most citizens are ideologically innocent: indifferent to
standard ideological concepts, lacking a consistent outlook
on public policy, in possession of genuine opinions on only
a few issues, and knowing damn little.
—Donald R. Kinder

THIS is the textbook view of citizens' capacity to reason about
politics—knowing little and caring little about political ideas
and public affairs; equally likely to take either side of an issue;
their opinions arranged higgledy-piggledy, sometimes consistent for a pair of issues, nearly as often not. Admittedly, this
is a vivid expression of the textbook view. "Knowing damn
little" is on the strong side. And, of course, not everyone sub-
scribes to the textbook view. But qualifications noted, it is
widely agreed that citizens do not or cannot understand fundamental political ideas. They are, in the fashionable phrase,
"innocent of ideology."

It is likely to appear perverse, therefore, to declare that

this is a study of ideological consistency. But it only appears perverse because it has tacitly been supposed that citizens must organize their ideas relying on their own resources. That is not so. The ecology of the party system affords partisans an opportunity to make ideologically coherent choices without exceptional effort on their part. The parties do the work for them. They organize the alternatives on offer along ideological lines, and just so far as the choice set is already ideologically organized, it is easier for voters in general, and a party's supporters in particular, to make consistent choices among them.

There are thus two claims. The first is a negative one. It has seemed out of ordinary citizens' reach to have a coherent view of politics because it has been supposed that they must coordinate their ideas relying on their own resources. This claim is false not for a few but for a very large number. It is false just so far as political parties structure the ecology of politics. Whether and to what extent citizens can benefit depends, therefore, on the goodness of fit with the party system.

What does goodness of fit require? It is necessary to give this question a pretty precise operational answer, and, what is more, an answer whose validity can be checked by anyone with access to a standard data set. This is not the time and place to introduce a novel method or measurement procedure. So I shall identify three specific conditions of goodness of fit: citizens must identify with one of the parties; they must identify with the ideological outlook that their party is identified with; and they must know the ideological reputations of the parties.[1]

I do not claim, and I do not believe, that they are necessary conditions for holding an ideologically coherent view of politics. But I do claim, and shall show, that the three are sufficient and that large numbers—large defined by any reasonable standard—satisfy them. This is the story that I am going to tell. I believe that, once told, rather than appearing perverse, it will have the virtue of appearing obvious.

IDEOLOGY: HIERARCHY AND DEDUCTION

It is well to observe that, when ordinary citizens are said to be "innocent of ideology," the term "innocent" is semantic camouflage. The contention is not that citizens are uncorrupted by ideology. The claim instead is that they do not have what it takes to be ideologically coherent. What, more exactly, does it mean to claim this?

The claim can be divided into three parts. (1) The political ideas of citizens are not organized along politically coherent lines. This part of the claim has wide but not universal support.[2] Hence the second part of the claim: (2) The political choices of the overwhelming number of citizens, even when consistently liberal or conservative, are not grounded in a commitment to liberalism or conservatism as political ideologies.[3] And the reason is, (3) only a comparative handful are able and motivated to make the effort to master the higher-order abstractions that underpin liberalism and conservatism and therefore deserve to be considered capable of ideological reasoning. All in all then, far and away most students of public opinion and politics reject the idea that ordinary citizens tend to make choices along ideological lines for ideological reasons.

Why is the "innocence of ideology" claim accepted as true, even self-evidently true? The canonical definition of ideology is a "cognitive structure capped by concepts of a high order of abstraction" that "permits the person to make sense of a broad range of political events."[4] So conceived, an ideology is a coherent "structure that subsumes content of wide scope and diversity [and therefore] must be capped by concepts of a high order of abstraction."[5] This definition, with its emphasis on "cognitive structure" and "abstraction," has a formidably antiseptic character. Converse provides a formulation that gives it more life. Political ideologies, he writes, feature "some superordinate value or posture toward man and society, involving premises about the nature of social justice, social change, 'natural law,' and the like. Thus a few crowning postures—like premises about survival of the fittest in the spirit of social Darwinism—served as a sort of glue to bind together many more specific attitudes and beliefs, and these postures are of prime centrality in the belief system as a whole."[6]

Preferences for vividness in writing style aside, both formulations bring out the signature features of an ideology: hierarchy and deduction. An ideology is a cognitive pyramid.[7] At the top of the pyramid are a small number of capstone abstractions. At the bottom of the pyramid are a large number of issue preferences. In between are mid-level beliefs and values. So conceived, ideological reasoning is top to bottom, from abstract to specific, deductive rather than inductive.

How, asked Converse and his colleagues, can citizens, knowing and thinking as little as they do about politics and public affairs, possibly master the "elegant abstractions of a high-order" at the core of political ideologies like liberalism and conservatism? So framed, to ask the question is to answer it. Of course, the average citizen lacks the training and sophistication, not to omit the incentives, to master an abstract system of ideas, to reason from first principles, to know what goes with what, still less to understand why.

Putting empirical flesh on the bones of this conception of ideology, Converse and his colleagues asked a representative sample of people to express in their own words what they liked and disliked about the political parties and the presidential candidates running under their banners. Respondents were free to evaluate the parties and candidates on ideological grounds, if considerations of ideology spontaneously came to mind. Only 2.5 percent of a representative sample could be classified as "ideologues"—that is, people who showed that they "rely in some active way on a relatively abstract and far-reaching conceptual dimension as a yardstick against which political objects and their shifting policy significance over time were evaluated."[8] Testing the limits of generosity, a further 9 percent could be classified as "near ideologues," that is, people who invoked abstract concepts but in "a peripheral way" or had only a shallow understanding of their meaning.[9] All in all, on the basis of systematic evidence as well as common sense, the conclusion to draw was obvious: only a "precious few" have even a limited understanding of the "relatively abstract and far-reaching conceptual dimensions" that make up ideologies like liberalism or conservatism.[10] For an overwhelming number of citizens, the concepts of liberalism or conservatism are outside their reach.

It is instructive to learn whether citizens, when giving their views about the parties' and presidential candidates' strong and weak points, spontaneously bring up ideological considerations. But happening to do so or not to do so is not a test of possessing or failing to possess an ideological outlook, or of being capable or incapable of using it appropriately.

Consider a hypothetical example. Imagine yourself saying to a friend, "I feel that the Republican Party has become too conservative." Your friend might or might not agree with you, since a normative and not solely an empirical judgment is being asked for. But she would recognize what you meant by "too conservative"; indeed, you would feel comfortable even if, at that moment, she could not give you a specific example of the Republican Party becoming too conservative. But, you may reply, she would understand what you meant because she, like you, is not an ordinary citizen. After all, people who read books like this tend to have an uncommon interest in politics and friends with similar ones.

So imagine another conversation, this time with a person selected at random from the population at large. If she heard you say, "The Republican Party is more conservative than the Democratic Party," what are the odds that she would know what you mean? This was also a question that Converse investigated. Fully one out of every two people can both get the heart of the matter right and correctly apply the terms to the parties.[11] Using a concept correctly—not giving a dictionary definition of it—is the test of understanding it.

AN ECOLOGICAL THEORY OF IDEOLOGICAL CONSISTENCY[12]

The premise of previous studies of ideology and mass publics is that citizens, if they are to develop an ideological outlook on politics, must master an abstract system of ideas. The premise of the approach I am suggesting is that citizens get help from the political environment. Help comes in more than one form, but the one I will focus on is the party system.

There is nothing original in a suggestion that political parties help voters in general, and their supporters in particular, to organize their preferences. Parties are salesmen. They label their wares. They advertise them. They hawk them, most unabashedly at election time. This, the motivational role of political parties, has been the focus of research. What I have become persuaded of, however, is the value of taking a step back, to bring into view how parties organize the choice set as well as motivate the choice process. Hence this study's leitmotif: it is because the alternatives on offer are organized on politically coherent lines that citizens can make politically coherent choices.

The particular alternatives on offer at any given moment are a response to the preferences of voters, partly.[13] But the organization of the choice set, what goes with what and why, depends upon institutions as well as individuals, and above all, the institution of electoral competition through the medium of political parties. They bear the burden of drawing things together. It is not necessary that a party's promises be coherent. It is important that they avoid appearing incoherent; better still, that they have—or appear to have—a unifying rationale. Hence the value of parties' developing ideological reputations, lowering the information costs to voters by representing competing brands, so that their labels "carry relatively precise meanings. The Democratic candidates tend to be liberal, and Republicans tend to be conservative."[14]

This is the intuition on which I rely. By coordinating and labeling the choice set in ideological terms, political parties solve for a large bloc of the electorate the problem of inadequate knowledge. It is not necessary for their supporters to master an abstract system of ideas. It is necessary that they know a crucial—but radically simple—piece of information—that the Republican Party is more conservative than the Democratic Party.

Inductive vs. Deductive Reasoning: The Role of Similarity

"An 'ideology' may be seen," to reprise *The American Voter*'s canonical definition, "as a cognitive structure that subsumes content of wide scope and diversity [and therefore] must be capped by concepts of a high order of abstraction."[15] Ideological reasoning, it follows, is reasoning from first principles, of deducing the specific from the abstract. Deductive reasoning on this order requires a high degree of political sophistication. As Luskin puts it, "Sophistication and abstraction are theoretically and empirically intertwined."[16]

Deduction from first principles may be the route for political theorists. Similarity is how the rest of us learn what goes with what. Social welfare policies differ in detail, most obviously in who benefits—senior citizens, the unemployed, minorities, schoolchildren. But they pose a recognizably similar choice: between government assistance and individuals' providing for themselves. Deduction from first principles is not required. Substantive similarity does the job: How about increasing government spending for people in need? Increasing spending for the unemployed? For protecting the environment?[17] Knowing what goes with what is not difficult just so far as like goes with like. Substantive similarity goes only so far, however. Disparate policy demanders make disparate demands. Clusters of independent policies develop. Then parties make strategic use of ideological labels. So both parties brand pro-life and limited government as conservative, pro-choice and activist government as liberal, and by virtue of sharing the same label, quite different policies are, as it were by definition, brought into ideological consistency.[18]

Institutions, Ideological Reputations, and the Problem of Inadequate Knowledge

From the outset, the labels "liberal" and "conservative" have been recognized as the keys to coherence. On this, Converse was explicit: "The single word 'conservative' [or liberal] used to describe a piece of proposed legislation can convey a tremendous amount of more specific information about the bill—who probably proposed it and toward what ends, who is likely to resist it, its chances of passage, its long-term social consequences, and, most important, how the actor himself should expect to evaluate it if he were to expend further energy to look into its details."[19] The question then is: what must citizens know to make use of the terms liberal and conservative as ideological constructs? Up until now, it has been supposed that the way to answer this question is to treat it as a problem in cognitive psychology. Thus, Converse's answer was: "First, the actor must bring a good deal of meaning to the term, which is to say that he must understand the constraints surrounding it. Second, the system of beliefs and actors referred to must in fact be relatively constrained."[20] Kinder and Kalmoe, updating Converse, say "general engagement with politics."[21] But though different in detail, the two answers cash out the same. The cognitive requirements of understanding liberal and conservative as ideological constructs rule out all but a small fraction of the electorate. As Kinder and Kalmoe put it, "Genuine ideological identification—an abiding dispositional commitment to an ideological point of view—turns out to be rare. Real liberals and real conservatives are found in impressive numbers only in the higher echelons of political society, confined to the comparatively few who are deeply and seriously engaged in political life."[22]

Why do so few citizens have a grip on ideological reasoning? The answer seems self-evident. They don't know what they need to know. This is known as the problem of inadequate information. The problem has seemed insoluble. Far and away most citizens lack either the capacity or the motivation to learn what they need to learn to engage politics on an ideological basis. This way of putting things sounds straightforward enough, but it puts the problem the wrong way around. The right place to start to understand political reasoning is not the psychology of citizens but the constraints of politics—especially the institution of electoral competition through the medium of political parties.

Political parties have incentives to develop policy reputations. In fact, the policies bundled together in response to a medley of policy demanders, party activists, and campaign contributors, themselves make up a medley. Moreover, parties occasionally, albeit rarely, find it is to their benefit to reverse their position on an issue.[23] But it is not to a party's advantage to appear incoherent. Quite the contrary. Parties may stand for more than one thing. But they cannot stand for patently opposing things. And for purposes of marketing, it is handy to have a trademark to attach it to their offerings. Hence the use of ideological labels, liberal/conservative, left/right, as policy trademarks. All of which is to say that it is not citizens who "must bring meaning" to the ideological terms liberal and conservative, as Converse would have it.[24] It is the parties that must and do bring meaning to them.

Grant that it is less difficult for citizens to organize their preferences along ideological lines when the parties do so for them. But is there still not a challenge in grasping the "meaning" of liberalism and conservatism, of understanding how they differ and in what ways the parties embody them? Here the originating metaphor for ideology is helpful. As a member of the Legislative Assembly in 1791 wrote in a somewhat partisan spirit, "The places on the left side that had been occupied in the Constituent Assembly by the true champions of liberty were invaded and seized by the most spirited innovators. . . . A far larger number of enlightened men of moderate opinions, reputed to be wise and almost indifferent observers, hastened to the center, where their mass and packed ranks might, by dint of numerical weight and strength, take on in their own eyes the appearance of an immense majority, comforting to them in their timidity. There remained to conscientious friends of the constitution only those places on the right which in the previous assembly had been occupied by the defenders of the *ancien régime*."[25]

Left-right, this spatial metaphor, is key to solving the problem of inadequate information. There has seemed no way that citizens could acquire enough knowledge about politics to make ideologically consistent choices, paying as little attention to politics as they characteristically do. But it is not necessary to know the particular point on the left-right continuum at which either the Republican or the Democratic party is located. Know that the Republican Party is to the right of the Democratic Party, and you know what you need to know to make ideologically consistent choices.[26] And who is most likely to make use of this piece of information? Citizens who identify with the ideological outlook of the party that they identify with—Democrats who see themselves as liberal, Republicans who see themselves as conservative.[27]

Two things, then, are key to ideological reasoning: identify with the outlook of the party that you identify with and know the relative ideological locations of the parties, and you are in a position to engage political issues on an ideological basis.

Continuity and Change

The standing presumption is that the portion of the electorate whose thinking about politics is ideologically grounded is more or less constant—namely, small. And so it will be if ideological consistency requires that citizens develop an "elaborate, close-woven, and far-ranging structure of attitudes." Suppose, however, that ideologically grounded reasoning is instead tied to political parties and their commitment to ideological identities. Then there is an institutional basis for coherence and continuity. Parties occasionally flip their positions on an issue as the Democratic and Republican parties have done on issues of race, the former moving from conservative to liberal, the latter from liberal to conservative.[28] But they do not flip their ideological identities.

The Democratic Party has been the party of liberalism, the Republican Party the party of conservatism. And it is not a matter merely of continuity of labels. Since at least the New Deal, the dominant programmatic cleavage in American politics has been over the scope of government on issues of social welfare. Without exception, the Republican Party has taken the conservative side of the social welfare policy agenda, the Democratic Party the liberal side.

Continuity of commitment paradoxically provides a basis for ideological polarization. The parties' ideological reputations, as it were, precede them. Even in eras when they are not trumpeting their ideological identities, substantial numbers of citizens know who is who, ideologically speaking.[29] But the parties, or better those who act in their names, have a strategic choice in calling attention to their ideological identities. Over the past thirty years, they have both diverged ideologically and emphasized their ideological divergence.

Partisan polarization at the elite level brings in its wake an array of responses at the mass level, among them an increase in the persuasive impact of party endorsements and reinforcement of aversive reactions to the opposing party.[30] And what is the result, all in all? Depending on the degree to which they accentuate or mute their ideological identities, parties can increase or decrease numbers of partisans who meet the two conditions for ideological consistency: knowing the ideological reputations of the parties and identifying with the ideological outlook that their party is identified with. Ideological polarization at the elite level is the key to engaging politics on ideological terms as a mass phenomenon.

IDEOLOGICAL CONSISTENCY

Ideological Orientation and Issue Preference

On the argument that I am making, the likelihood of making ideologically grounded choices depends on satisfying two conditions: identify with a party whose ideological outlook matches yours and know the ideological reputations of the parties. The crucial point is that the largest portion of the public easily meets these two conditions. In the 2012 presidential election, for example, two-thirds of the public identified with one or the other of the two parties; just under two-thirds of them identified with the ideological outlook of their party; and virtually all of them knew the ideological identities of the parties.[31] All in all, in 2012, just over half of the general public met the two conditions—identifying with a party whose outlook matched theirs and knowing the ideological reputations of the parties.[32]

One-half of the public near enough with the means and motivation to make ideologically grounded choices is not the "thin slice" of the electorate Converse spoke of. It is a large chunk of it. And it is my claim, outlandish as it may sound, that a hallmark of those who make it into this half of the electorate is the ideological coherence of their political ideas.

What, operationally, does it mean to say that political preferences are ideologically coherent? The question has more than one answer. For the purposes at hand, it is a tight connection between a person's conception of him- or herself as a liberal (or conservative) and his or her consistently taking liberal (or conservative) positions issue after issue. How tight is tight? There is no way to avoid being arbitrary. I am not aware of a study reporting correlations between ideological identification and issue position consistently greater than .30 for the general public.[33] So I will snatch a number out of thin air, and define a tight connection between ideological outlook and issue position as a correlation of .5 or greater.

Table 2.1 reports the strength of association between general ideological orientation and positions on specific issues conditional on whether respondents identify with a party and its outlook and on whether they know the ideological reputations of the parties—that is, know that the Republican Party is more conservative than the Democratic Party. This allows us to separate pure independents, partisans who either do not identify with the ideological reputation of their party but know their ideological reputations or the other way around; and ideological partisans—that is, party identifiers who identify with the ideological outlook that their party is identified with and know the ideological reputations of the parties. The upper panel of Table 2.1 reports issues measured in the seven-point paired alternative format pattern, while the lower panel shows issues measured in a different format: whether government spending for a policy should be increased, decreased, or stay the same.[34]

Consider government health insurance. Respondents are asked their preference between two alternatives—government insurance and private insurance. For those who identify with the ideological outlook of their party and know the ideological reputations of the parties, the correlation between ideological identification and issue position is stunningly large: .70. A subjective judgment, to be sure, but stunningly large is a judgment anyone familiar with previous estimates of the

Table 2.1 Conditions of ideological consistency: Social welfare

	Government jobs _Know ideological reputations_		Government services _Know ideological reputations_		Government health _Know ideological reputations_		Limited government _Know ideological reputations_	
	No	Yes	No	Yes	No	Yes	No	Yes
Independents	-.06	.15	.00	.28	.00	.26	-.03	.23
Non-sorted partisans	.07	.13	-.04	.15	.04	.18	-.01	.19
Sorted partisans	.03	.58	.33	.67	.10	.70	.12	.72

	Child care _Know ideological reputations_		Environment _Know ideological reputations_		Social Security _Know ideological reputations_		Welfare _Know ideological reputations_	
	No	Yes	No	Yes	No	Yes	No	Yes
Independents	.07	.20	.12	.30	.00	.11	.02	.30
Non-sorted partisans	.00	.17	.03	-.15	.05	.02	.05	.13
Sorted partisans	.31	.43	.22	.56	.02	.22	.04	.53

Note: Data are Pearson product moment coefficients. Response format for top row of issues is a 7-point option, for the bottom row a 3-point option.
Source: 2012 American National Election Study (ANES).

magnitude of linkages in mass belief systems will agree with. In contrast, for the other half of the public, the correlations between ideological identification and issue position run from zero to minimal in size.

The results for ideological consistency on the issues of government service, government responsibility for jobs, and a commitment to limited government are virtually identical. On the one side, there is a tight connection between ideological identification and issue position for party identifiers who identify themselves with the ideological outlook of their party and know the ideological reputations of the parties ($r = .67$, .58, and .72, respectively). On the other side, there is at most a minimal connection and more typically scarcely any at all for everyone else.

The pattern of results for levels of government spending, shown in the lower panel of Table 2.1, is the same, though the tightness of the connection between ideological identification and issue position is noticeably less tight; indeed, for one issue, Social Security, it is scarcely visible (.22). This is a particularly nice illustration of limitation of correlation coefficients. Their magnitude is conditional on the variance in the variables being correlated.[35] As it happens support is skewed systematically in favor of spending for most social welfare policies. Social Security is an extreme example: conservatives are as allergic as liberals to the idea of cutting government spending on it. The result is to constrain artificially the magnitude of the association between ideological identification and issue positions for social welfare issues asked in the format of whether government spending should be increased, be decreased, or remain about the same.

The appropriate measure is the unstandardized, not the standardized, coefficient. Happily, results using unstandardized regression coefficients for the government spending measures parallel those for the measures in the top panel of Table 2.1 in both pattern and magnitude.[36] Why not present the results that more strongly favor the argument I am advancing? Because a shared understanding of the magnitude of correlation coefficients in this research field has developed over the decades. Public opinion researchers will immediately recognize that product-moment correlation coefficients of .70 and .73 are extraordinary in size; they will not so immediately or uniformly recognize that an unstandardized coefficient of .53 or .63 are similarly out of the ordinary.

The social welfare agenda is the primary policy agenda that the parties contest. But they divide also over social values issues. By social values issues, I mean most concretely gay rights and abortion, but also a broader division in the general public over whether traditional morality is threatened and what place it in any case should have in contemporary society.[37] For illustration's sake, consider the positions that respondents take when given a choice between whether gay and lesbian couples should be allowed to legally marry; they should be allowed to form civil union but not legally marry; or there should be no legal recognition of a gay or lesbian couple's relationship. For partisans who share the overall ideological outlook of their party and know the parties' ideological reputations, there is a tight connection between their ideological identification as a liberal or a conservative and the position that they take on whether or not gays should be allowed legally to marry ($r = -.61$). For everyone else, the correlation between ideological identification and issue position runs from trivial to minimal (Table 2.2).[38]

The pattern is the same for gay adoption, gay marriage, and commitment to traditional morality: for partisans who know the ideological reputations of the parties and identify with the ideological outlook of their party, there is a strong connection between ideological identification and issue position; for everyone else, connections vary from trivial to minimal.

The results in Tables 2.1 and 2.2 are consistent and big, and they should be surprising to public opinion analysts who contend that, a thin slice of the electorate aside, citizens are innocent of ideology. Our results demonstrate, instead, that for partisans who are in ideological synch with their parties, which amounts to half of the general public, there is a tight linkage between ideological identification and issue position (median correlation = .64).[39] May I say that I expected that the linkage between ideological orientation and issue preferences would be tight for partisans who know and identify with the broad outlook of their party? I had no idea that it would be this tight.

I have used the expression "stunningly large" to characterize the magnitude of the correlation coefficients for ideological partisans.[40] It is fair to ask whether the characterization "stunningly large" is apt. The magnitude of a correlation coefficient is contingent on multiple considerations, among them the type of coefficient, measurement error, and item variance. I have searched for a standard yardstick. Converse's contrast of levels of "constraint" in elite and mass samples is as close as I can come.

Table 2.2 Conditions of ideological consistency: Social values

	Gay adoption Know ideological reputations		Gay marriage Know ideological reputations		Abortion Know ideological reputations		Traditional values Know ideological reputations	
	No	Yes	No	Yes	No	Yes	No	Yes
Independents	-.15	-.15	-.06	.16	.13	.05	.05	.34
Non-sorted partisans	-.09	-.15	-.10	.23	.00	.18	.05	.28
Sorted partisans	-.14	-.50	.11	.61	.06	.53	.36	.69

Source: 2012 ANES.

Conceptually, constraint is defined as functional interdependence of beliefs. Operationally, it is defined as success in predicting the position that respondents take on one issue, knowing their position on another. Pearson product-moment coefficients are the most familiar, and therefore the easiest to use as a benchmark to judge how exceptionally large are the coefficients in Tables 2.1 for ideological partisans. However, product-moment coefficients are systematically larger than tau b, the coefficient used by Converse.

How do the constraint results for ideological partisans compare with those reported by Converse for political elites and the general population, using the more conservative estimator? For his sample of political elites, the median coefficient for domestic issues is .57; for the general population, .23.[41] For our sample of ideological partisans, the median coefficient for domestic issues is .43; for the remainder of the general public, .22. The preferences of ideological partisans are not as constrained as those of congressional candidates, which cannot be a surprise; but they are in the same broad neighborhood, which should be a surprise.[42] There is not as large a gulf between how tightly organized are the preferences of ideological partisans as there is for those of the rest of the public as between elites and the electorate as a whole, which cannot be a surprise. The preferences of ideological partisans are not as tightly constrained as those of congressional candidates, to be sure. But congressional candidates are the epitome of constrained belief systems. By any down-to-earth standard, the belief systems of ideological partisans are tightly constrained.

Knowledge of the Parties' Ideological Reputations
or Knowledge of Politics in General

Previous research has rightly highlighted the motivational role of parties—the extent to which they serve as reference groups for their adherents. My objective, instead, is to distinguish between their role in motivating choice and their role in organizing the choice set. The latter is as elemental as the former. I have focused on the parties' positive role, in organizing the alternatives on offer so that a large portion of the public is in a position to hold an organized view of politics, with relatively little effort. There are other roles that parties play, however, and they are less obviously positive. Just so far as the choice set is defined through them, the number of alternatives is reduced. Their role in excluding issues and concerns from consideration is an elemental constraint on democratic representation. Parties do not have complete agenda control, and they are in any event a medium through which policy demanders, interest groups, and other actors do much of their work. But it would be a great failing to focus on the role of parties in facilitating consistency of choice without at least mentioning their role in constraining the scope of it.

It is their role in coordinating the choice set that is the focus of this study, however. The claim on the table is that parties afford their supporters a path to follow to be ideologically consistent by organizing the alternatives on offer on ideological lines. Grant that this is so. The question that arises immediately is, at what cost? How much do they need to know in order to take advantage of the parties' organization of the choice set?

The answer I have given is that what they need to know—whether the Republican Party is more conservative than the Democratic Party—is very easy to learn. But there is an obvious objection. Knowing the ideological reputations of the parties may matter, not because there is something especially telling about this particular piece of information, but because the people who know it are also the people who know a lot of other things about politics. Hence the need to determine whether it is knowing the parties' specific ideological reputations or being broadly knowledgeable about politics that matters.

To arbitrate between these two possibilities, Table 2.3, Panel A, presents measures of association between ideological identification and positions on social welfare issues, conditional on knowledge of the parties' ideological reputations and/or knowledge about politics in general.[43]

Look first at the importance of general political information. It is plain that overall ideological orientation becomes increasingly relevant with increasing general knowledge of politics. For the least well informed, the correlation between general ideological outlook and issue position on the social welfare agenda is .17; for those with a middling level of knowledge, it is .45; for the comparatively best informed it is .68. An impressive result, and one entirely consistent with previous research.

Which makes the interior of Table 2.3 all the more instructive. The two internal rows show the extent to which the linkage between overall outlook and issue position on the social welfare agenda is conditional on possessing a specific piece of information—the parties' ideological reputations.

Table 2.3 What kind of information counts more?

Panel A. Social welfare policies

		General political information					
		Lowest				Highest	
Knowledge	Don't know	.03	.13	.03	.07	.09	.06
of ideological	Know	.36	.47	.54	.68	.70	.60
reputations							
of the parties							
		.17	.41	.45	.64	.68	

Panel B. Traditional values agenda

		Lowest				Highest	
Knowledge	Don't know	.18	.12	.01	.24	.38	.12
of ideological	Know	.17	.50	.54	.61	.71	.50
reputations							
of the parties							
		.17	.41	.45	.61	.71	

Source: 2012 ANES.

Look at the highest scoring fifth on the measure of general knowledge of politics. If the subjects also know the ideological reputations of the parties, the correlation between ideological self-identification and positions on specific social welfare issues is striking, $r = .70$. But if they do not know the ideological reputations of the parties, even though they otherwise are quite well informed about politics compared with their fellow citizens, the correlation between general outlook on politics and specific positions on issues is equally striking for just the opposite reason. It is trivial, r = .09. Scarcely a whiff of a connection between ideology and issue position for those who do not know the ideological reputations of the parties; the closest of connections, for those who do, is what the results in Table 2.3, Panel A, show.

Panel B repeats the analysis of Panel A, substituting positions on the traditional values agenda for those on the social welfare agenda. The results in all essentials are the same, albeit less dramatic. General knowledge of politics again appears vitally important at first glance. But on closer examination, knowing or failing to know the ideological reputations of the parties clearly is pivotal. Look at the difference knowing or failing to know this specific piece of information makes for the best informed. If the top fifth of subjects do not know the ideological reputations of the parties, the correlation between general ideological identification and issue position on social values is .38; if they do know it, the correlation is .71.

In Table 2.3, Panels A and B both show that ideological consistency hinges on knowing that the Republican Party is to the right of the Democratic Party. It is not how much information one has about politics that appears to matter. It is whether one has a particular piece of information. The piece of information needed for consistency of political ideas—knowing that the Republican Party is to the right of the Democratic Party—is easy to learn. And it is just because it is easy to learn this—three out of every four knew it in 2012—that ideological consistency is a hallmark of the political thinking of a large bloc of the electorate.

Ideological Polarization

Estimates differ on how many in the general public are capable of engaging politics in ideological terms. Some put it as low as 2.5 percent, some as high as 20 percent. But no one has claimed that the portion of the public capable of ideological reasoning is large.[44] The proportion of the public that is, so to speak, ideologically competent, though variable over time, is not capacious at any point in time. It is relatively inelastic because citizens' cognitive competence is limited and because their level of attention to politics, though variable over short periods, is limited over extended ones. For either or both reasons, the accounts of ideological reasoning currently on the books are incapable of accounting for change in a substantial degree.

At the elite level, the ideological cleavage between the parties has progressively widened over the past three decades.[45] Those who act in their name have become more loyal soldiers in the ideological cause of their party, and furthermore, the causes they champion have become more extreme.[46] Ideological polarization has become a defining feature of contemporary American politics. In turn, as parties have put a spotlight on their ideological identities, the ranks of ideological partisans have greatly increased.

Table 2.4 tracks the percentage of the electorate consisting of party identifiers who identify with the overall ideological identity of their party and know the ideological identities of the parties. Through the 1970s and 1980s, the proportion hovers around one out of five—in the neighborhood of other high estimates of ideologically oriented voters.[47] But the ranks

Table 2.4 Proportions over time of
partisan types and independents

	Ideological partisans (%)	Traditional partisans (%)	Pure independents (%)
1976	25	59	15
1984	30	59	11
1992	33	55	12
2004	43	46	11
2012	47	40	15

of ideological partisans in the electorate multiplied as the parties polarized ideologically at the elite level.[48] By 2012, just under half of the electorate were ideological partisans, twice as many as in 1976.

Grant that the proportion of party identifiers who are in ideological synch with their parties increased as the parties polarized ideologically. Does it follow that the importance of ideology, of their image of themselves as liberal or conservative, also increased? It can reasonably be argued that, though ostensibly qualifying as "ideological" partisans, party identifiers who nominally were ideologically in synch with the party system in the 1970s and 1980s were not as ideologically grounded as their successors. They may have put more weight on their ideological self-identification in choosing positions on an issue than fellow party identifiers back then, but not as much as their counterparts when the parties polarized ideologically.[49]

It is not implausible; indeed, it may seem more credible than the alternative, namely, to suppose that the issue preferences of ideological partisans were as ideologically grounded in an era where the party system was comparatively depolarized ideologically. Still, the ideological ecology of the American party system has been fixed since at least the New Deal, with the Democratic Party the party of the left, the Republican Party the party of the right. Know this, share the overall outlook of your party, and you have the information and guidance you need to line up with your party on the core issues that the two parties contest. It follows, if this second line of reasoning is right, that although the proportion of party identifiers who know and share the overall outlook of their party will change over time as the salience of ideology in the competition between the parties varies, and the tightness of the linkage between ideological orientation and issue positions for partisans who do know and share the overall outlook of their party will be more or less constant over time.

Table 2.5 reports the extent to which issue positions on a composite measure of issue liberalism-conservatism are tied to ideological identification for ideological partisans, traditional party identifiers, and pure independents over the years from 1984 through 2012.[50] Unstandardized ordinary least squares (OLS) coefficients are reported so that the magnitudes of coefficients are not variance sensitive.[51]

Again, as in Table 2.1, the contrast between ideological partisans and the rest of the public is dramatic. For the latter, there is only a threadbare connection between ideological identification and issue liberalism-conservatism. For ideological partisans, the absolute values of the coefficients suggest an increase in the significance of ideological considerations as American politics polarized ideologically. In 1984,

Table 2.5 Ideological identification and issue
liberalism-conservatism by orientation to parties
(ANES unstandardized coefficients)

	1976	1984	1992	2004	2012
Ideological partisans	.621	.444	.516	.607	.670
	(.04)	(.05)	(.03)	(.03)	(.013)
Traditional partisans	.266	-.047	.068	.134	.180
	(.06)	(.05)	(.04)	(.08)	(.03)
Pure independents	.201	.043	.170	.314	.185
	(.113)	(.09)	(.08)	(.224)	(.05)

Source: ANES Cumulative File. The index of liberalism-conservatism
combines responses to the government jobs, government health
insurance, and government services, though the last was first asked
in 1982.

the coefficient is .444. Over the period, it steadily increases
in size. At the end of the period, in 2012, it is .670. Then again,
postulating trends based on only a few data points is a mug's
game. Note the size of coefficient in 1976, .621.

TAKEAWAYS

There is a common roadside hazard in political science of
winding up in disagreements that are only disagreements
about words. The original and still customary conception of
ideology—a "cognitive structure capped by concepts of a high
order of abstraction" that "permits the person to make sense
of a broad range of political events"—was right and proper.[52]
More to the point, it has been immensely useful. Conceiving
of ideology in these terms helped bring into view a whole way

of thinking about public opinion and politics. But it is not the only way to conceive ideology. An alternative, and I believe more telling, test of understanding a concept is using it correctly. On this standard, large blocs—not a thin slice—of the electorate have a good grip on liberalism-conservatism. But if this is not to be just an argument about definitions, it is more than fair to ask, in what ways is this conception of ideology useful?

The most obvious benefit is that it points the way to a solution of the seemingly insoluble problem of inadequate knowledge. How could an ordinary citizen have an ideologically coherent system, it has been asked over and again, given how little he or she knows about politics?

The problem of inadequate knowledge is insoluble on the assumption that it is the citizen who "must bring a good deal of meaning to the term[s]" liberal and conservative. Even citizens who know an uncommon amount about politics do not know all that much. But the whole point is that citizens do not need to rely only on their own resources. The ecology of the party system affords the guidance they need. The parties organize the choice environment. They define what goes with what. They label their policy packages. Indeed, they double-label them. Republican equals conservative, Democrat equals liberal, making obvious both *what goes with what* and *why*. By organizing and labeling the choice set ideologically, the parties radically reduce information costs. It is necessary to know that the Republican Party is more conservative than the Democratic Party. If you do not know that, you cannot make ideological sense of contemporary politics. Know it and you can.[53] It is also necessary that liberalism or conservatism matters enough to you that you identify with the party that is identified with your ideological outlook. But this is all you have to do to be in a position to engage politics on an ideological basis. Citizens who see themselves as liberals or conservatives, who understand the ideological organization of the party system, who consistently and systematically line up on the liberal or conservative side of issues, are not an anomaly. In contemporary American politics, engaging politics on ideological terms is a mass phenomenon.[54]

Opposing blocs of the public now clash on an ideological basis. They do so because the parties have starkly identified themselves as vessels of liberal and conservative creeds. The result: in 2012, partisanship is different for a large portion of the electorate partisanship than in the 1950s.

Conventionally, party identification is supposed to represent an emotional attachment with minimal policy content. Party identification, so conceived, reflects the force of habit and blind feeling. But for more people, partisanship now represents something quite different—a political identity.[55] These are party supporters who identify themselves with the ideological outlook that their party is identified with. For the largest number of Republicans, to be a Republican is to be a conservative. For fewer but still a great number of Democrats, to be Democrat is to be a liberal; to be a liberal is to be a Democrat.

Here, I fear, is a paradox. I doubt that any student of contemporary American politics would deny that partisanship is a political identity for a large bloc of the electorate. To the extent that partisanship is a political identity, it does not make sense to treat party identification and ideological identification as separate and distinct. It has, however, been standard practice for fifty years to do so, to run regressions to determine whether more of the explanatory variance should be attributed to party identification than to ideological identification, the implicit assumption being that party identification represents pretty much the same thing, an emotional attachment with minimal policy content, for pretty much everybody. Hence the taken-for-granted juxtaposition of party identification gauging the force of habit, and emotion and ideology the influence of ideas and cognition. Paradox or irony, I am not entirely sure, since I suspect the habit of treating party identification as mere habit and emotion, without policy content, will be a habit that is extremely hard to overcome.

That would be a pity. Many partisans of today are like their counterparts of the 1950s, emotionally bound to their party for reasons that have little to do with policy. But unlike in the 1950s, the largest number of party identifiers are bound to their party by a conception of themselves as liberal or conservative rightly committed to their party because it is committed to liberalism or conservatism.

CHAPTER THREE

Myrdal's Insight: The Politics of Race

Nᴏᴛ much more than a half century ago, progress on the issue of race seemed a chimera. In the South, both law and custom denied blacks the right to vote, to attend the same schools as whites, to live where they wished and could afford, to have the same opportunities to get a job or to get promoted, to drink from the same water fountains as whites — to mention only some chains clamped on black Americans. And if segregation was the law in the South, it was the practice in the North, if not to the same degree, then to a fair approximation.

Looking back, progress may appear to have been inevitable. It did not seem so then. Southern legislators had a chokehold on the House and Senate. Northern as well as Southern whites would in any case massively resist change — as they did when the Supreme Court ruled for school desegregation. Opposition, unapologetic, unremitting, bloody, comes first to mind, naturally. But to those who can call back live memories of America before the civil rights movement forced its way forward, the telltale mark of the times was the absence of attention to the treatment and conditions of life of black Americans.[1] Support for racial equality expressed itself in little more than a hope that moderation would prevail, ultimately—whenever that might be.

A PUZZLE

It is now supposed, virtually as a matter of common sense, that white Americans will no longer publicly express derogatory stereotypes of blacks for fear of being judged racist. Vividly put, "Openly expressing prejudice is like blowing second-hand cigarette smoke in someone's face: it's just not done any more in most circles, and if it is, people are readily criticized for their behavior." As far as I can determine, the principal evidence for this claim were the so-called Scientific American studies.[2] These studies traced trends in racial attitudes through the 1950s, 1960s, and 1970s. The change was dramatic: a collapse of public support for de jure discrimination in public accommodations, transportation, and employment. The conclusion that was drawn: "White America has become, in principle at least, racially egalitarian."[3]

It seemed obvious that whites would no longer express blatantly derogatory judgments of blacks, for fear of appearing racist; so obvious that for decades there were no systematic surveys of racial prejudice. But it did not follow that, because white Americans no longer supported legal segregation, they no longer were racially prejudiced. On the contrary, studies of pluralistic ignorance warned that the racially intolerant overestimated the number of fellow Americans who, like them, were racially intolerant; while the racially tolerant underestimated the number who were, like them, racially tolerant.[4] The result: even when the racially intolerant were a minority, they believed they were the majority; conversely, the racially tolerant, although in fact a majority, believed they were in the minority. Why then, we reasoned, suppose that the minority would feel they were no longer free to say what they believe—and believe that most others believe—namely, that blacks were not as good as whites? No doubt some would not say they would be inhibited; no doubt, in special circumstances, still more. But the power of social norms against racial prejudice had been greatly exaggerated, we suspected.[5]

The only way to determine whether our suspicion was justified or not was to give whites an opportunity to be nasty toward blacks. So in our first study of race and politics, we included a number of blatantly derogatory statements about blacks. The prediction was that many whites would agree with them. And they did. Two examples: In a representative sample of the liberal, affluent, well-educated San Francisco Bay Area, one out of three agreed that "most blacks have a chip on their shoulders" and that "black neighborhoods tend to be run down because blacks simply don't take care of their property," while one out of five agreed that "blacks are more violent than whites."[6] Nor is the readiness of white Americans to publicly make derogatory judgments about blacks a thing of the past. In the 2012 American National Election Study (ANES), almost one out of every two whites judged whites to be more intelligent than blacks and more than one out of two declared them to be more hardworking; and in their 2006 American Racial Opinion Survey, Huddy and Feldman found that "between one fifth and one quarter of white Americans . . . think that racial differences in intelligence of fundamental genetic differences between the races explain some or a great deal of the economic and education gap between blacks and whites."[7]

It would be a mistake to believe that all who dislike and disdain blacks will say so. It is a bigger mistake to doubt that there are large numbers of whites who feel quite comfortable making blatantly derogatory remarks about blacks to perfect strangers.

But there is a puzzle. There is only a modest connection between racial prejudice and the positions that whites take on issues of race.[8] This makes no sense. When a white person declares that blacks are innately inferior, he means what he says. And what risk is there to him in saying that he doesn't agree with affirmative action? Or that people who are on welfare should stand on their own two feet? Prejudice and opposition to government help for blacks should be strongly related. But they aren't. Why not?

The Asymmetry Hypothesis

Politics should be the starting point in analyses of political choice—that is the overarching hypothesis of this study. How does it apply to race? The politics of race determines the relevance of racial prejudice to politics. Consider a conservative's perspective on a proposal to increase government spending for more job training programs for black Americans. Should she support or oppose it? Just so far as she is politically conservative the decision is easy. Of course she should oppose it. This is yet one more example of setting up one more government bureaucracy, run from Washington, no more likely to be successful than previous efforts but guaranteed to cost a barrel full of money. This is what, as a conservative, she knows. She may think well of blacks. But that is no reason for her, as a conservative, to support a prototypically liberal proposal.

Now, consider how a proposal for more government job training programs for black Americans should look to a liberal. Job training programs are a gold-star liberal policy. As a liberal, he should support it. But suppose he dislikes blacks—not an absurd assumption since there is not exactly a shortage of bigots on the left. He has a conflict: his liberalism pulls him toward support for the policy; his aversion to blacks pushes him away.

What follows if this reasoning is right? The impact of prejudice is ideologically asymmetrical. The further to the left people are, the more central the role of prejudice in shaping their policy choice; the further to the right, the more peripheral—a prediction that has twice been confirmed on independent samples and using different measures of prejudice.[9]

The result: the politics of race is deeply ideological but asymmetrically cohesive. The right is united in opposition to liberal policies on race. The left is divided. Just so far as egalitarianism has a hold on liberals and Democrats, they have reason to support liberal policies on race. But just so far as prejudice has a hold on liberals and Democrats, they have reason to oppose them. A paradox follows. Prejudice is more common on the right than the left, but politically more consequential on the left than on the right.[10]

Or so I believed. Myrdal's *An American Dilemma* points the way to seeing how our research exaggerated the magnitude of the impact of prejudice on the political left.

THE RISE AND FALL OF
AN AMERICAN DILEMMA

For those born after the crest of the civil rights movement, it is hard to grasp the full measure of the subjugation of blacks in the South. For myself, I know no better way to catch a glimpse than to call to mind the other classic study of the South, John Dollard's *Caste and Class in a Southern Town*.[11]

Caste and Class was published just seven years before Myrdal's *An American Dilemma*. The concept of caste helps capture the enormity of racial subordination in the South. The root of caste is *käst*. *Käst* also is the root of castaway. Castaways, perhaps because it calls to my mind an image of human beings as disposable, has a singular resonance. However that may be, the word "caste" captures the social and economic imprisonment of blacks. A member of an economic class has the possibility of change in her circumstances. A member of a caste cannot change position, whatever her gifts, whatever her efforts. To recognize that blacks were not merely an underclass, but a caste, captures the perpetuity of subordination.

Or rather the apparent perpetuity of racial subordination. For Dollard's account was right descriptively, wrong dynamically. Myrdal recognized that the status quo in the South was enforced by a myriad of forces: "personal and local interests; economic, social, and sexual jealousies; considerations of community prestige and conformity; group prejudice against particular persons or types of people; and all sorts of miscellaneous wants, impulses, and habits dominate his outlook."[12] But he had a deep insight. The institution of racism was an assault on the moral ideals of Americans. White Americans would "*twist and mutilate their beliefs of how social reality actually is.*"[13] But twist and turn as they will, white Americans could not in the end escape. The legal and social subordination of blacks could not be squared with their consciousness of their commitment to the American Creed, to the ideals of equality, liberty, and fair play. Hence the famous lines: "The American Negro problem is a problem in the heart of the American. It is there that the decisive struggle goes on. . . . Though our study includes economic, social, and political relations, at bottom our problem is the moral dilemma of the American."[14]

Myrdal's concept of the American Creed was well known to students of race in America a generation ago. But the backstory of the concept was little known then, and is all but unknown now. After the fall of Norway in 1940, Myrdal, with his own country of Sweden at risk of invasion by Hitler, felt it his duty to break off work on the project of race in America and return home. There he and his wife Alva worked to stiffen resistance to Nazi influence, to deflate conviction of the certainty of a German victory, and to rally Swedes in support of democratic values.

It is a minor historical irony that it was only in marshaling his imaginative resources to inspire his fellow Swedes to defend freedom that the master idea of *An American Dilemma*—the idea of an American Creed—came to Myrdal's mind. It is a more instructive point that he chose to call it the American Creed. He did so not because he believed there was something peculiarly American about a commitment to the values that made up the Creed—liberty, equality, and fair play. Commitment to those values was as deeply grounded in Sweden as in America.

What set Americans apart was the *consciousness* of their commitment to the values of democracy. It was the consciousness of their commitment that gave their moral ideals a propulsive force. Myrdal believed, in consequence, that the values of the Creed would ultimately prevail over racial subjugation. Victory was not preordained.[15] *An American Dilemma* was not merely a description of the conditions of blacks in America. It was a call to action.

Publication of Myrdal's *An American Dilemma* coincided with the upsurge of the modern civil rights movement. Myrdal's belief in the propulsive force of the moral ideals of the American Creed served as a fundamental premise for the movement's narrative. It provided a framework for the stories and pictures reported first by the Negro press, and then by the national media, that brought home the courage and suffering of civil rights activists and the violence and immoralism of Southern authorities.[16] In the end, the result was success— success on a scale unimaginable when Myrdal's work first appeared. Who, as late as the summer of 1963, foresaw passage of the Civil Rights Act of 1964 outlawing racial discrimination, still less passage of the Voting Rights Act of 1965, committing the federal government to preventing racial discrimination in voting?[17]

This moment, you might well think, was a triumphant vindication of Myrdal's optimism about the positive forces working for racial equality. But in a heartbeat, as it seemed then, race riots erupted, first in Watts, then in city after city, summer after summer. Simultaneously, demands for "Black Power" pushed the pledge of nonviolence to the background; the outlaw glamour of Malcolm X eclipsed the moral appeal of the traditional leaders of the civil rights movement; while study after study, culminating in the Kerner Report, documented the persisting impoverishment of black Americans, their virtual imprisonment in urban ghettos, injustice in the justice system, and the failure of institution after institution, the educational system chief among them, to provide equal opportunity to black Americans. Against this background of crisis and failure, Myrdal became a poster child for the vacuous optimism of liberalism. His monumental work, *An American Dilemma*, was dismissed, in a stinging phrase, as "Sunshine sociology."[18]

The dismissal of Myrdal's work as "Sunshine sociology" is a prize example of a triumph of self-righteousness over scholarship. Myrdal never supposed that racial progress was assured. On the contrary, *The American Dilemma* ends with the declaration: "History is not the result of predetermined fate. Nothing is irredeemable until it is past. The outcome will depend upon decisions and actions yet to be taken."[19] Above all, *An American Dilemma* remains the definitive account of the shackles of social, economic, and political discrimination in the America of the 1930s and 1940s. But my interest is looking forward, not backward.

Myrdal got right the most important forces disrupting the status quo of the America of the 1930s and 1940s, above all, the economic and demographic transformations in progress in the South: the constriction of agriculture, and the opening of factory work in the North and the Great Migration that followed. He also got right that blacks are agents, not just subjects, of history. How many other students of race relations, it is worth asking, were willing to put pen to paper to predict the Negro rebellion in the South?[20] He also got right the propulsive force of moral ideals. But the most important thing that Myrdal got right was that there is a conflict over race.

Myrdal supposed that the conflict was a conflict within the minds and hearts of white Americans as they wrestled with the contradiction between the ideals of the American Creed and the facts of bigotry, segregation, and exploitation. Some white Americans wrestled with this contradiction, but over the past half century, the primary lines of conflict have been political, between liberalism and conservatism, the Democratic Party and the Republican Party. The character of that conflict is my concern.

PREJUDICE AND THE POLITICS OF RACE

The Meaning and Measurement of Prejudice

The essential nature of prejudice, many believe, has changed. The old racism was one thing. The new racism is a different beast. In the most influential conceptions, this new racism — xenophobia, Islamophobia; the label reflects the immediate circumstance — is tied to the nature of the larger society in which it has found support: late capitalism in some formulations, the Protestant ethic in others.[21] It is possible that investigation of the empirical connections between contemporary racism and the structure of the modern societies will prove fruitful. What has proved to be a dead end is the assertion that, *as a matter of definition*, racism and American values are conjoined. In the case of longest standing in the new racism research programs, that of symbolic racism/racial resentment, the phenomenon itself has been continually redefined in response to ongoing empirical results; indeed, redefined so often and so much that it now means the opposite of what it first meant.[22]

The strategy here accordingly is first to isolate what conceptually constitutes prejudice, then investigate empirically its causes and consequences. Figure 3.1 reproduces a brace of definitions of prejudice. At first glance, the diversity of diagnostic symptoms of prejudice is striking.[23] Stereotyping is one; rigidity another one; misinformation yet another. On a second look, what is striking is the consistent appearance of a particular theme: "a failure of human-heartedness," "a pattern of hostility," "hostility or aggression," "hostility," "an unfavorable attitude," "attribution of negative characteristics." Prejudice, on every conception, is bound up with antipathy. More expansively, prejudice comprises a persisting, predictable, systematic readiness to dislike, belittle, punish, exclude, or push away members of a minority. The more derogatory, hostile, or aversive a person's reactions to a minority, the more prejudiced he or she is.

Accordingly, my colleagues and I have developed a measure of the willingness of white Americans to attribute derogatory characteristics to black Americans, asking them how well a number of adjectives describe most blacks: in particular, "aggressive or violent," "lazy," "boastful," "irresponsible," "complaining."[24] Of course, it wouldn't do to ask respondents whether they would agree with one after another after another

Definition 1: "Prejudiced attitudes … are irrational, unjust, or intolerant dispositions towards others. They are often accompanied by stereotyping. This is the attribution of supposed characteristics of the whole group to all its individual members." (Milner 1975, 9)

Definition 2: "It seems most useful to us to define prejudice as a failure of rationality or a failure of justice or a failure of human-heartedness in an individual's attitude toward members of another ethnic group." (Harding et al. 1969, 6)

Definition 3: "An emotional, rigid attitude, a predisposition to respond to a certain stimulus in a certain way toward a group of people." (Simpson and Yinger 1985, 21)

Definition 4: "Thinking ill of others without sufficient warrant." (Allport 1954, 7)

Definition 5: "Ethnic prejudice is an antipathy based upon a faulty and inflexible generalization. It may be felt or expressed. It may be directed toward a group as a whole or toward an individual because he is a member of that group." (Allport 1954, 9)

Definition 6: "An unsubstantiated prejudgment of an individual or group, favorable or unfavorable in character, tending to action in a consonant direction." (Klineberg 1968, 439)

Definition 7: "A pattern of hostility in interpersonal relations which is directed against an entire group, or against its individual members; it fulfills a specific irrational function for its bearer." (Ackerman and Jahoda 1950, 2–3)

Definition 8: "Hostility or aggression toward individuals on the basis of their group membership." (Buss 1961, 245)

Definition 9: "Group prejudice is now commonly viewed as having two components: hostility and misinformation." (Kelman and Pettigrew 1959, 436)

Definition 10: "A set of attitudes which causes, supports, or justifies discrimination." (Rose 1951, 5)

Definition 11: "An unfavorable attitude toward an object which tends to be highly stereotyped, emotionally charged, and not easily changed by contrary information." (Krech, Crutchfield, and Ballachey 1962)

Figure 3.1. What is prejudice?

Here are a few words that people sometimes use to describe blacks. Of course, no word fits absolutely everybody. How well does each of these words describe most blacks?

Dependable
Intelligent in School
Aggressive or Violent
Lazy
Smart with practical, everyday things
Law Abiding
Boastful
Determined to Succeed
Hardworking
Friendly
Irresponsible
Keep up their Property
Complaining
Good Neighbors

Figure 3.2. Measure of racial prejudice

disparaging characterization of blacks. Our strategy was to bury the negative adjectives in a long list of positive adjectives. This would soften the impact of the derogatory descriptors, we reasoned. We employed twice as many positive as negative characterizations. The positive adjectives, I would emphasize, were not meant to be measures in their own right. What did it take to say that blacks are, say, dependable? This was, in political science parlance, cheap talk. The purpose of the positive adjectives was to put respondents in a position, by ticking off some positive adjectives, to feel free to express negative feelings toward blacks without appearing to be racist.

Figure 3.2 lists all fourteen adjectives, in the order in which they were asked.

The Asymmetry Result Reinterpreted

A useful starting point is to determine whether or not prejudice still has a stronger impact on the political left than on the right. Table 3.1 presents the results of two independent tests of the asymmetry prediction, one taking advantage of the 2012 American National Election Study (ANES), the other of the 2012 National Race and Politics Study (NRAP).

As Table 3.1 shows, party identification is strongly associated with racial liberalism: the more strongly whites identify as Democrats, the more likely they are to support racially liberal policies; the more strongly they identify as Republicans, the more likely they are to oppose them. Prejudice is strongly associated, too: the more prejudiced whites are, the more likely they are to oppose racially liberal policies; the less prejudiced they are, the more likely they are to support them. No surprises here.

The key result is the ideological asymmetry of prejudice and political choice. The more strongly whites identify as Republican, the less important prejudice; the more strongly they identify as Democrats, the more important prejudice. This is true for the two independent samples; true also, and worth underlining, notwithstanding multiple differences between the measures of prejudice in the two studies. The takeaway: the original finding—that the impact of prejudice is politically asymmetrical, meaning stronger on the left, weaker on the right—is reconfirmed.

Table 3.1 Prejudice, party identification,
and racial liberalism

	Racial liberalism * (whites only)	
	2012 ANES	2012 RAP
Party ID	-.582 (.04)	-.471 (.03)
Prejudice**	-.414 (.02)	-.431 (.03)
Party ID × Prejudice	.427 (.06)	.302 (.06)
R^2	.219	.388

Racial policy preferences: Interaction of
prejudice and party identification

* Racial liberalism
   ANES = government help for blacks and for
treatment for blacks
   RAP = government help for blacks, for
treatment for blacks, and for preferential
treatment of blacks
** Prejudice
   ANES = difference between ratings of whites
and blacks on intelligence and hardworking
   RAP = 5 negative objectives

A Conjecture

Replication of a result is uncommon; repeated replication
across measures and samples is rare. But time and the election
of the first African American president of the United States
led to a rethinking of the problem. Was it possible that there

was good will toward minorities as well as ill will? Was it, to go a step further, possible that substantial numbers of white Americans, so far from having a negative view of black Americans, have a positive view of them?

When I say that someone has a positive view of blacks, I do not mean that she feels sorry for blacks, or believes that blacks are unfairly treated, or wishes blacks were better off. She may feel, believe, and wish all of this. I am far from dismissing sympathy and a sense of injustice as unimportant considerations in the politics of race.[25] But believing that blacks have been badly treated and deserve help is one thing. Thinking well of them—seeing them as responsible, decent, capable—is quite another. It is out of the ordinary to suggest that having a positive regard for blacks is a factor in the politics of race, I concede. It is therefore closer to the mark to characterize the idea that substantial numbers of white Americans think well of black Americans as a conjecture rather than a hypothesis.

Grant the possibility that substantial numbers of white Americans do not merely not think ill of black Americans but think well of them. What is the most useful way to think of the relation between positive and negative sentiments toward blacks? The simplest way to do this is to suppose there is a continuum running from most positive feelings toward blacks to most negative. As a practical matter, we can do a good job of ordering white Americans from most negative to most positive simply by combining negative and positive evaluations of blacks.

Simple usually beats complex, not least because simple tends to have the advantage of modesty in measurement assumptions. We need not assume that positive feelings are as strong as negative ones. It is necessary only that the evaluative continuum be bipolar, that is, run from negative to positive, and that the differences in affect be monotonic—that is, there is no presumption that those who are most positive in their evaluations of blacks are as positive as those who are most negative are negative. Moreover, we also can slough off the difference between ambivalence and indifference.

The aim is to gauge the relative impact of negative and positive evaluations of blacks on the political thinking of whites. But how should we think of the transition from negative to positive? As a zone of indifference, or as a cut point?[26] If a zone, how are its borders to be established? If a cut point, where is it to be located? It is not that these questions do not have answers. They do, many different answers, each about as plausible as the others. Which is to say that the choice between them is arbitrary, and therefore the results of analysis are arbitrary, too.[27]

The conjecture I want to explore is that thinking well of blacks, and not merely not thinking ill of them, matters. To do so requires a principled procedure for treating positive and negative evaluations separately. The minimal standard for determining whether the positive and negative adjectives are measuring different things is that they load on different factors. Confirmatory factor analysis yielded two factors with eigenvalues greater than one.[28] The five negative adjectives, but none of the positive adjectives, load significantly on one factor.[29] The nine positive adjectives, but none of the negative adjectives, load significantly on the other factor.

Measurement reliability, standardly gauged, is a function of the number of items in a measure and the degree of their intercorrelation. The measure of racial prejudice consists of the five negative items. To build a measure of similar length of the readiness to attribute positive characteristics to blacks, the nine positive adjectives were factor analyzed to identify the optimal five to use. The five items with the highest loading on the first factor were: dependable, intelligent at school, law abiding, determined to succeed, and hardworking. The five positive items were combined to form an Index of Positive Esteem, weighting each adjective equally.[30] We thus have two measures of equal length and comparable reliability to work with, a measure of prejudice operationally defined as a systematic readiness to attribute negative characteristics to blacks and a measure of positive esteem operationally defined as a systematic readiness to attribute positive qualities.

Customarily, finding two dimensions settles the question of whether a set of indicators is measuring one latent variable or two. But a conjecture that some substantial number of white Americans have a positive view of black Americans is unexplored territory. So I should like to raise the evidentiary bar.

If the two factors are substantively, and not merely statistically, distinct, then to some degree they must be measuring different things; which is to say that each is associated with attributes that the other is not. What are those attributes?

It is easy to say for negative evaluations of blacks. A signature characteristic of prejudice is a disposition to dislike, to belittle, to punish, to exclude, or to push away members of a minority. To the extent that a systematic readiness to attribute negative evaluations of blacks is different from, and not merely opposite to, a readiness to attribute positive evaluation, then

Table 3.2 Distinctive correlates of negative evaluations
of blacks: Mean-spiritedness

Sentiments	Negative affect	Positive affect
People make excuses for failure	.253	−.033
	(.025)	(.028)
Should distrust those who are different	.198	−.015
	(.020)	(.026)
Society too soft on the undeserving	.361	−.093
	(.026)	(.029)
Unsuccessful; have only self to blame	.191	−.097
	(.025)	(.028)
Measures of prejudice		
Anti-semitism	.367	.001
	(.025)	(.027)
Psychological tolerance	.370	−.075
	(.026)	(.029)

thinking ill of blacks should be distinctively tied to mean-spirited, judgmental, punitive orientation toward others.

Table 3.2 shows the results of regressing an array of harsh, judgmental orientation toward others on the measures of prejudice and positive esteem. Thinking ill of blacks, the results show, is distinctively tied to all the strands of this syndrome of harsh, judgmental, mean-spirited sentiments. Thus, high scorers on the Prejudice Index are markedly more likely than low scorers to be unsympathetic and dismissive of those who have not achieved as much as they would have hoped or liked, declaring, for example, that "Too many people are too quick to make excuses why they haven't succeeded in life." Nor can it be a surprise that high scorers on the Prejudice measure also are marked by a lack of faith in people in general, agreeing that "One should distrust those who act differently from most people." Even so, the misanthropic, punitive, judgmental tone of their sentiments is striking, as illustrated by their assertions that "One of the problems of today's society is that we are often too soft on people who don't deserve it" and that "People who don't do well in life usually have nobody to blame but themselves." In contrast, the Index of Positive Esteem Toward Blacks is either not associated at all or only trivially associated with all of these indicators of mean-spiritedness.

Thinking ill of blacks, the results in Table 3.2 show, distinctively keeps company with a family of aversive sentiments. But this carries us only half the distance to establishing that positive and negative evaluations of blacks are distinct. If positive and negative evaluations are indeed distinct factors, positive evaluations should be tied to a network of sentiments that negative evaluations are not.

What are these sentiments? Myrdal gave special emphasis, when picking out moral ideals as forces promoting racial progress, to sentiments of fair play and equality. On this reasoning, the Index of Positive Esteem should be distinctively tied to a disposition to care for, to assist, to reach out to, to be concerned for the well-being of others.

Table 3.3 shows the results of regressing the measures of prejudice and positive esteem on indicators of a disposition to reach out to, to embrace, to care for others, and to want them taken care of. Whites who think well of blacks stand out for

Table 3.3 Distinctive correlates of positive evaluations of blacks

Sentiments	Negative affect	Positive affect
Unequal chances a big problem	.008	.283
	(.003)	(.036)
Needy should be helped by others	−.045	.311
	(.026)	(.029)
Should always help less fortunate	−.090	.222
	(.020)	(.022)
More equal wealth would reduce problems	.059	.224
	(.034)	(.037)

their desire to assist and help others, asserting that "All people who are unable to provide for their basic needs should be helped by others." They also are more eager to see that those who are less well-off become better off, believing that "One should always find ways to help others less fortunate than oneself." For that matter, they stand out for their support of the proposition that "If wealth were more equal in this country we would have many fewer problems."[31] High scorers on the Index of Positive Esteem are also more likely to believe that "All people who are unable to provide for their basic needs should be helped by others." Prejudice, in contrast, is not significantly associated with any of these indicators of sympathy, compassion, and beneficence to others.

The conclusion to draw: notwithstanding their being highly correlated with one another, predispositions to evaluate blacks positively or negatively keep company with different sets of sentiments.

THE EXAGGERATION OF THE
IMPACT OF PREJUDICE

It is a psychological truism that the more whites dislike blacks, the less they like them, and vice versa. What then, one need ask, are the possible consequences of taking account of thinking ill of blacks but not of thinking well of them?

Equation 3.1 lays out a standard model of prejudice and racial politics:

$$Op = a + b_1P + b_2V + u$$

In this model, Op represents opposition to policies intended to help black Americans; a is a constant; b_1P is the coefficient indexing the impact of disliking and disdaining blacks; b_2V is a vector summarizing the influence of other relevant factors (for example, ideology, party identification, class, education); and u is the error term.

Equation 3.1 is the model estimated in previous studies of prejudice and racial politics. Our conjecture is that positive as well as negative evaluations matter. So far as that is so, there is a risk that previous research (very much including our own) has exaggerated the impact of prejudice on political choice, particularly on the left. For by omitting to take account of positive esteem for blacks, the variance associated with thinking well of blacks is attributed to thinking ill of them.[32] The result: the importance of prejudice is overestimated. Hence the need to estimate Equation 3.2, not Equation 3.1.

$$Op = a + b_1P + b_2E + b_2V + u$$

where Op represents opposition to policies intended to help black Americans; b_1P is a coefficient registering the impact of

Table 3.4 Prejudice party and racial liberalism (unstandardized coefficients)

	Democrats		Independents		Republicans	
Prejudice	-.407	-.284	-.333	-.222	-.156	-.115
	(.04)	(.05)	(.04)	(.05)	(.03)	(.04)
Positive esteem		.275		-.222		.07
		(.06)		(.05)		(.04)

prejudice; b_2E is a coefficient indexing the impact of esteem for them; b_2V is a vector summarizing the influence of other relevant factors; and u is the error term.

A centerpiece result of our research on race is the ideological asymmetry of the politics of race: the impact of prejudice on political choices is larger on the political left than on the right. Table 3.4 accordingly shows the impact on racial liberalism of feelings about blacks separately for Democrats, independents, and Republicans. For each of the three, the table reports, first, the increase in opposition to racial liberals for a one-unit increase in the level of negative feelings toward blacks, then in the next column, the increase in opposition to racially liberal policies for a one-unit increase in thinking ill of blacks plus the increase in support for them for a one-unit increase in thinking well of them.[33]

Consider Democrats first. The coefficient for prejudice, considered by itself, is a very substantial -.407. But if you look at the second column, which presents the results of taking account of esteem for blacks as well as prejudice against them, two things are clear. First, a sizeable portion of the variance attributed to thinking ill of them—on the order of a third— should have been attributed to thinking well of them. Second, the impact of positive sentiments toward blacks is equal in size, though of course opposite in direction, to that of negative sentiments toward them.

For independents, the same two observations hold— inflation of the impact of prejudice by virtue of failing to take account of positive regard and the off-setting impact of positive regard. There is a third observation to add, though. Consistent with the asymmetry hypothesis, the impact of both positive and negative sentiments on the policy choices of independents is smaller for independents than for Democrats. One might offer the same three observations about Republicans, but they are trivially true. For the impact of prejudice, though statistically significant, is tiny, while that of thinking well of blacks fails even to reach the conventional level of statistical significance. In a word, how Republicans feel about blacks, whether negative or positive, is irrelevant to the position that they take on racial policies. Republicans are homogeneously conservative, markedly more so than Democrats are homogeneously liberal, and as conservatives, they take conservative positions on racial policies.[34]

THE ASYMMETRY
HYPOTHESIS REEXAMINED

On the view that I am urging, to understand the role of prejudice in the political thinking of white Americans, it is necessary to begin with their stance toward politics. Republicans are overwhelmingly conservative in outlook. Asked whether they support or oppose affirmative action or more spending on welfare or expanding job training programs for blacks, their answer is no. How they feel about blacks is beside the point. It is only those who are open to supporting liberal policies on race who might be dissuaded from doing so by how they feel about blacks, and given how homogeneously conservative Republicans are on issues of government intervention to assist the disadvantaged, for practical purposes that is scarcely anybody.

That is the argument. But it presupposes that Republicans share a policy-relevant reason to make a common choice. It follows that when they do not have to hand an ideological reason to make a common choice, the door is open for their feelings about blacks to influence their choice.

The 2016 Republican presidential primary contest provides an opportunity to test this reasoning. By March 16, three candidates remained: Donald Trump, Ted Cruz, and John Kasich. Trump was capturing on the order of 40 percent of Republican primary votes.[35] On any reasonable interpretation, Trump presented Republicans with an opportunity to act on intolerance. Failure to find a connection between racial prejudice and support for Trump would undercut the reasoning underpinning the asymmetry hypothesis.

A survey was commissioned to put this new prediction to a test. The purpose of the study was narrowly targeted: to determine whether or not there was a connection between racial prejudice and support for Trump. Because its purpose was custom targeted, the survey design was custom tailored: one thousand Republicans, all white. They were interviewed in a narrow time frame, March 17 to March 25, 2016.[36] The fourteen-adjective measure of evaluations of blacks in the RAP study was repeated. Respondents were asked which

Table 3.5 Prejudice and Trump support: Republican primary study (unstandardized coefficients)

	Trump		Cruz		Kasich	
Prejudice	.329	.258	−.083	−.090	−.160	−.101
	(.06)	(.07)	(.06)	(.07)	(.05)	(.05)
Positive esteem		−.143		−.047		.119
		(.08)		(.07)		(.06)

Republican candidate they would most likely vote for—Ted Cruz, Donald Trump, John Kasich, another Republican candidate, or none.

Table 3.5 reports regressions of support for the three candidates on prejudice and positive esteem for blacks. Since the dependent variable is dichotomous, probit coefficients are reported. The results fit expectations. The more prejudiced Republicans were, the more likely they were to support Trump. And there was no offsetting influence of thinking well of blacks. Both negative and positive evaluations of blacks had nothing to do with support for Cruz. Positive evaluations of blacks and support for Kasich went together. In short, when it is relevant, prejudice counts for as much on the right as on the left.

A REFLECTION

Liberalism has been an engine for racial equality. Hence the irony of previous research showing prejudice to be politically more consequential on the left than on the right. The irony remains, but qualified. Our results show that negative evaluations of blacks count for more on the left. But so, too, do positive evaluations. The result: the impact of thinking ill of blacks is in good measure offset by the influence of thinking well of them.

You might suppose that this would be a welcome finding. For some it is. For others, it is anything but. The suggestion that substantial numbers of white Americans think well of black Americans—see them, that is, as responsible, capable, decent—is a provocation. A claim that some substantial numbers of white Americans think well of black Americans is interpreted as an effort to minimize the persisting problems of prejudice and discrimination. The reaction is one of anger or sarcasm. It is as though in pointing to a positive aspect of the politics of race, one is denying indelible features of America's racial history—slavery, Jim Crow, separate but equal.

The right reaction to this reaction is not entirely obvious, beyond denying that one is denying America's racial history. What I have come to is this. If the core claim—that a substantial number of white Americans have positive attitudes toward black Americans—is right, there will be other, and I expect still better ways, to demonstrate that it is right.[37]

However that turns out, the hallmark of the politics of race is a clash of opposing forces at multiple levels. This was Myrdal's insight, and it applies, among many places, to sentiments about blacks. As thinking ill of blacks undercuts support for liberal policies on the left, thinking well of them reinforces it. Failing to appreciate this led me to exaggerate the importance of prejudice in shaping choices on liberals and Democrats.

AFTERWORD: THE REDEFINED MEANINGS
OF THE CONCEPTS OF SYMBOLIC
RACISM AND RACIAL RESENTMENT

David Sears and Donald Kinder have led the most influential research program on prejudice and American public opinion. Their concentration of purpose is unmatched. So, too, is the consistency of their results. In every study that they have carried out, they have concluded that this particular form of racism—they variously call it symbolic racism or racial resentment—is "by a far margin . . . the most important" factor shaping the political thinking of white Americans on issues of race.[38]

Their measure of racism is the only measure that generates results consistent with this claim. Not surprisingly, then, it has been the focus of criticism, principally on issues of measurement.[39] Sears in particular has been exemplary in responding to criticism conscientiously and in detail.[40] But pro and con, measurement has been the attention magnet. The result has been to take attention away from the conceptualization of symbolic racism/racial resentment.

What is symbolic racism? In a research program carried out over so long a period of time, it is both inevitable and appropriate for researchers' thinking to develop and change as results from later studies succeed those of earlier ones. But the definition of symbolic racism has not been modified at the margins. It has twice been transformed. It now means the opposite of what it originally meant.

Figure 3.3 identifies the three life stages of the concept of symbolic racism/racial resentment—(1) a fusion of antiblack

The Original Definition

1a. "Symbolic racism ... we define as a blend of antiblack affect and the kind of traditional American moral values embodied in the Protestant Ethic." (Kinder and Sears 1981, p. 416)

1b. "the finest and proudest of traditional American values, particularly individualism." (Sears 1988, p. 54)

The Second Definition: The Reconceptualization of Individualism

2a. "Individualism *within* prejudice." (Kinder and Mendelberg 2000, p. 60, italics in original)

2b. "Black individualism," that is, "the sense that Blacks violate individualistic values." (Sears and Henry 2003, p. 264)

The Third Definition: The Rejection of the Traditional Values Claim

3a. ". . . is separate and distinct from American values." (Kinder and Dale-Riddle 2012, p. 177)

3b. "Symbolic racism: A blend of conservatism and racial antagonism." (Sears and Henry 2003, p. 263)

Figure 3.3. Definitions of symbolic racism/racial resentment

affect and traditional American values, above all, individualism; (2) racialized (or black) individualism; and (3) a fusion of antiblack affect and political conservatism.[41]

Symbolic racism at the outset was defined as a fusion of antiblack affect and commitment to traditional American values. Individualism was the prototypical traditional value — individualism understood as embodying the values of self-reliance, hard work, and self-discipline. A fusion or conjunction of antiblack affect and commitment to traditional American values, this was how symbolic racism was first defined, and as best that I can tell, it is how even specialists in race and American politics believe it is still defined.

The first definition was shipwrecked by the focus on individualism, however. If individualism is an integral component of symbolic racism, measures of individualism and symbolic racism will be highly related. In fact, a battery of studies demonstrated that they are minimally related.[42] What to do? On the one hand, it was not possible to defend the claim that individualism conventionally understood was an integral component of symbolic racism. On the other hand, it was not possible to concede that the concept of symbolic racism did not incorporate individualism without sinking their research program.

There was one way forward: redefine the concept of individualism. Individualism no longer meant a "traditional American moral values embodied in the Protestant Ethic." It now meant, in Kinder and Mendelberg's phrase, "individualism *within* racism" (definition 2a).[43]

What does it mean to say "individualism *within* racism"? It is no longer commitment to the value of individualism, to holding oneself to standards of self-reliance and self-discipline. The claim now is that standards of self-reliance and self-discipline provide a means for vilifying blacks. So Kinder and Mendelberg contend, "At the center of prejudice today is a deeply felt resentment that blacks choose to live in ways that repudiate individualist virtues, abiding commitments to hard work, discipline, and self sacrifice."[44] Sears and Henry take the same line, agreeing that it is not individualism per se that fuels prejudice nowadays, but rather a bastard form of individualism, "Black individualism" they call it, "the sense that Blacks violate individualistic values" (definition 2b).[45]

But two more problems emerged. The first is tautology.

Here are two items. The first is: "Most blacks who don't get ahead should not blame the system; they really have only themselves to blame." The second is: "It's really a matter of people not trying hard enough; if blacks would only try harder, they could be just as well off as whites." Which item comes from the black individualism measure, which from the symbolic racism measure? Either could be in either measure. Correlating a measure of symbolic racism with a measure of black individualism comes down to correlating a measure with itself. And what is being measured? A readiness to stereotype blacks as lazy and self-indulgent. There is nothing symbolic about this, nothing new about this "new" racism. Some of the old stereotypes—that blacks are innately inferior—are less common (which is not at all the same thing as saying that they have disappeared). But the insistence that blacks are inferior, that they don't measure up, hasn't disappeared at all.

Which creates a contradiction. Symbolic racism/racial resentment is supposed to be a compound of antiblack affect and commitment to traditional American values. But if measures of symbolic racism/racial resentment are measures of a belief in the inferiority of blacks, then they are measuring the opposite of a core American value, namely, a belief in equality. To his credit, Sears is very much alive to this issue, pointing to evidence that symbolic racism is bound up with *anti*-egalitarianism, and then noting that this result, if reconfirmed, "would alter our view of symbolic racism . . . [and] would imply that resistance to racial change is more rooted in genuine resistance to equality than is implied by our original emphasis on perceptions that blacks violate nonracial individualistic values such as ambition, hard work, and delayed gratification."[46] Just so: the more racially resentful, subsequent analyses show, the more elitist, not the more egalitarian.[47] As Sears feared, resistance to racial change is rooted in a failure to internalize core American values, not in acceptance of them.

Hence the necessity for a third round of radical redefinition. Symbolic racism initially was defined as a conjunction of antiblack affect and traditional American values. Now, traditional American values are not a component of symbolic racism/racial resentment. According to Kinder and Dale-Riddle: "First, racial resentment and American values are only modestly associated. Views on self-reliance, equality, and limited government, on the one hand, and racial resentment, on the other hand, are typically significantly correlated, but the correlations are never large. Resentment, as we define and measure it here, is *separate and distinct* from American values" (definition 3a).[48]

"Separate and distinct" from American values totally contradicts the original conception of symbolic racism as blending antiblack feeling "with the finest and proudest of traditional American values" (definition 1a).[49] Sears and Henry go a step further, declaring that symbolic racism is "a blend of conservatism and racial antagonism" (definition 3b).[50] Conservatism, and this is vital, is not "simply a surrogate for traditional values."[51] It is political conservatism: identifying as a Republican and identifying as a conservative.[52] Defining symbolic racism as "a blend of conservatism and racial prejudice" totally contradicts the original claim that symbolic racism and conservatism are separate and independent.[53]

Originally defined as fused with traditional American

values, most importantly, the Protestant ethic, symbolic racism/racial resentment is now "separate and distinct from American values." Originally defined as separate and independent from political conservatism, it is now defined as identification with the Republican Party and a conservative outlook. The names of the phenomenon remain the same: symbolic racism/racial resentment. But the phenomenon has been redefined. It now means the opposite of what it originally meant.

CHAPTER FOUR

The Fear of Mass Politics

ASS and elite are the building-block concepts of empirical democratic theory. In the standard portrayal, average citizens' knowledge about politics and public affairs is threadbare; their political beliefs minimally coherent, indeed, often self-contradictory; their support for core democratic values all too likely to crumble in the face of a threat, real or imaginary. In contrast, the politically active and influential have a fund of political knowledge to draw on; their ideas are coherently connected one to another; their commitment to the values of a democratic politics, though imperfect, is far stronger and more principled than the mass public's. Ordinary citizens are the Achilles' heel of democratic institutions, the politically active and influential their guardians. This is without exception the judgment of the classic studies of mass politics.[1]

To the best of my knowledge, this picture of political elites and mass publics is descriptively accurate. It is also deeply misleading. A fear of mass politics is justified. What is missing is a recognition of the risks of elite politics.

THE POLITICS OF CIVIL LIBERTIES[2]

It is good manners to credit Tocqueville with the insight that democratic stability is predicated on societal consensus.[3] Societies require, he wrote, that "the minds of all citizens [are] rallied and held together by certain predominant ideas. . . . When a great number of men consider a great number of things from the same aspect, when they hold the same opinions upon many subjects, and when the same occurrences suggest the same thoughts and impressions to their minds."[4] It is admittedly not altogether clear just what are these "same thoughts and impressions to their minds" that provide a foundation for democratic politics. Minimally, they must include the idea of a democratic politics as a political ideal. More approximately, it is a conception of the Bill of Rights—a popularized, or if you prefer, vulgarized—version, but one that expresses the plain sense of core democratic principles— that people have the right to say what's on their mind, that their vote should count for as much as anyone else's vote, that everyone is equal before the law, and so on.

The systematic study of public opinion exposed the idea of a societal consensus on democratic rights as democratic myth. True enough, the general public overwhelmingly supports the principles of democratic politics when they are stated in the abstract. But in his classic study of civil liberties,

Stouffer showed that, confronting groups that they perceive as threatening or controversial, large numbers of citizens—indeed, sometimes large majorities of them—would openly support out-and-out violation of their rights.[5]

The rights of communists were most at risk then. Less than a third of Americans in Stouffer's study were willing to let a communist speak in their community.[6] This result, though chilling by itself, does not convey the shock of his findings. An example: asked whether "a clerk in a store" should be fired if he is a communist, 68 percent of the public said yes.[7] This is no more than an inch away from saying that one should fire grocery clerks if they are communists. For that matter, though the focus of Stouffer's study naturally was communists—an analysis of the hysteria about communist subversion was the point of his study—the grounds for concern go far deeper. At least it could be argued that there were communist spies. For that matter, Russia was a threat. But what was most chilling about Stouffer's findings—and what has fallen out of memory—was the scope of opposition to the rights of groups that were not a focus of public concern, that manifestly were not a threat to law and order, let alone to national security, whose only offense was being unpopular. It is one thing, at the height of the Cold War, to perceive communists to be a threat. But what justification can be given for perceiving atheists to be as great a menace as communists?[8]

Who, then, stands up for civil liberties in a crisis? The politically active and influential. Both Stouffer and McClosky showed in their classic studies that the politically influential more consistently stand by core democratic rights—freedom of speech, procedural rights—in the heat of specific controversies than does the general public. And what is as striking is the liberality of the definition of the politically active and influential—local officials, national convention delegates, trade union activists—a whole medley of citizens who are distinguished not necessarily by high office but merely by participation in the affairs of their communities. But politically powerful or merely community minded, by virtue of their involvement in politics, they are exposed to the norms of a democratic politics. So they both learn the norms and learn to respect them, if not to win the approval, then at least to avoid the censure, of their peers.

It may seem as though, in times of normal politics, the difference between the commitment of political elites and ordinary citizens toward civil liberties is of no consequence. That is an illusion of optimism. For there is plenty of tinder in mass publics ready to light up; hence the flash fires over, to point to a recent example, transgender individuals' use of bathrooms. Still, crisis politics brings out the full significance of the difference between elites and masses in support for civil liberties. The public remains ready to approve democratic principles qua principles. But now, in danger or believing themselves to be in danger, they put public safety and order over individual rights. Fortunately, the argument runs, because of their deeper understanding of and stauncher commitment to core democratic values, political elites provide a shield protecting the rights of groups and ideas that are regarded as dangerous or, even, are merely unfamiliar. The conclusion to draw: the political elite are the guardians of civil liberties, the custodians of the democratic creed.

Because the claim is that political elites provide a bulwark protecting democratic values, I will call it the Thesis of Democratic Elitism. It is worth remarking how the Thesis of Democratic Elitism fits the standard template in the study of public opinion. Again, the distinction drawn is between the mass public taken as a whole and the politically active and influential taken as a whole. Again, the difference drawn between the two is so sharp as to constitute a difference of kind, not merely of degree. And again, I would add, the root problem with this contrast of elite and mass public is a neglect of the ideological and partisan cleavages within both elite and mass publics.

Some issues of civil liberties and civil rights are settled. But others are the stuff of politics. How far should authorities be allowed to go in analyses of email to combat terrorists? What limits, if any, should be placed on public demonstrations if there is a threat of violence? On what grounds should police be allowed to stop and search suspects, and what protections should there be against unreasonable search and racial profiling? Is showing violence against women a form of pornography? Should transgender people be restricted to restrooms of their birth gender? Should a business be allowed to decline to serve customers on the grounds of sincerely held religious beliefs?

The specific issues have changed, but the ideological framework of the party system has stayed the same. The Democratic and Republican parties line up on opposing sides of issues of civil liberties election after election, one identifying itself as the champion of the liberal cause, the other as the champion of the conservative cause. Partly the sides of the issues they choose to back, still more the issues they choose to press, are tactical choices. There is no necessary logical connection between economic conservatism and religious fundamentalism. But neither is it entirely an accident that they meet in the Republican Party; no more than it is simply an accident that feminism and a concern with economic inequality meet in the Democratic Party.

It of course is no surprise that, among the politically active and aware, left and right line up on contested issues of civil liberties and civil rights. But what about the mass public? To what extent do they line up in opposing ideological camps on issues of civil liberties and civil rights? The question makes no sense if you believe that the ordinary citizen cannot engage politics on an ideological basis. We have seen that positions on domestic issues of a large swath of the public are organized on liberal-conservative lines and grounded in an understanding of oneself as a liberal or a conservative. But it is one thing for the general public to know and to conform to ideological positions on issues of social welfare. Clashes over the scope of government and individual responsibility have been at the center of the electoral battle between left and right since at least the New Deal. It is another thing for them to know and conform to ideological positions on issues of civil liberties.

The Charter of Rights study in Canada showed that, in the general public as well as the political elite, supporters of the party of the right and supporters of the party of the left consistently take opposing sides on issues of civil liberties.[9] On the limits of wiretapping; censorship; the rights of those who have been arrested; standards for reasonable search; the limits that should be imposed on public demonstrations; the grounds on which a state of emergency may permit a suspension of civil liberties—supporters of the party of the right systematically choose a narrower conception of the rights of citizens and a broader one of the responsibilities of government, while supporters of the party of the left do just the opposite. The ideological cleavage over democratic rights is deeper among the politically sophisticated than in the general public. Nonetheless, the cleavage between left and right among both elites and the mass public is unmistakable.

The results of a study of attitudes toward civil liberties in Canada lack the persuasive punch of a comparable study in the United States, I concede. Fortunately, the results of a still larger study in the United States are strikingly parallel to the Charter of Rights study in Canada. McClosky and Brill demonstrate in two independent studies that, in the mass public as among political elites, using a variety of measures of liberalism-conservatism, conservatives consistently, systematically score lower than liberals on a carefully validated scale of civil liberties.[10]

The ideological, and therefore partisan, bases of issues of civil liberties and civil rights are the key to the politics of rights. It is perfectly true that the *average* level of support for civil liberties among the politically active *taken as a whole* is higher than the *average* level of support among the public *taken as a whole*. But it is not the average of Democratic and Republican legislators combined that signals the direction that decisions on civil liberties will go. If the party of the left wins, governance will favor a broader conception of the rights of citizens. If the party of the right wins, governance will favor a broader authorization of the power of the state.

A key question then is, how deep does the divide on civil

liberties and civil rights between liberals and conservatives go? The cleavage within elites on the left and those on the right, McClosky and Brill show, dominates the difference between elites and the public. An example: liberals are twice as likely as conservatives to score high on an overall measure of support for civil liberties (89 percent compared with 44 percent). Conversely, conservatives are many times more likely than liberals to score low (19 percent compared with 1 percent).[11]

Suppose, to take a further step, you conduct a thought experiment. You have a choice between electing a sophisticated, politically aware conservative, or a citizen, selected at random, who identifies herself as liberal. Your priority is to protect, and if possible to enlarge, the scope of civil liberties. Which candidate should you pick? On the usual grounds, which contrast elites, taken as a whole, and the mass public, taken as a whole, your preferred candidate should be the sophisticated, politically influential conservative, not Jane Q. Public who happens to identify herself as a liberal.

McClosky and Brill's results give exactly the opposite counsel. All you know of the ordinary citizen is that she was picked at random from the general population and that she identifies herself as liberal. On McClosky and Brill's results, the ordinary citizen who is liberal is almost twice as likely to score at the high (or tolerant) end of the civil liberties scale than a politically engaged conservative (54 percent compared with 31 percent). Conversely, politically aware and articulate conservatives are nearly three times as likely to score at the low (or intolerant) end of the civil liberties scale than an ordinary citizen who is liberal (37 percent compared with 13 percent).[12]

Where does that leave us? Political scientists have drawn the conclusion that, because the politically influential are more likely, on average, to support civil liberties than the average citizen, political elites provide a bulwark protecting democratic values in political crises. They are, in McClosky's eloquent phrase, "the major repositories of the public conscience and . . . carriers of the Creed."[13] But this holds only if the politics of civil liberties is ignored. Representative government is party government. Elect the party of the right, and there will be readiness to place a higher priority on assurance of public safety and order than expansion of individual rights; elect the party of the left, and there will be a greater readiness to place a higher priority on expansion of individual rights over public safety and order.

Cautionary warnings are called for. It would be a great mistake to presume that issues of individual rights should always take priority over those of public safety. And it would take optimism on a heroic scale to infer, from the research results at hand, that issues of civil liberties would be in safe hands if citizens were picked at random to be attorney general, provided only that they were liberal in political outlook. But it takes an equally outsized neglect of the actual politics of civil liberties to skate over, as previous research has, the political significance of the clash of values between political parties competing for public power.

This is, I believe, a point worth more consideration than it has received.

Political Demagogues: Mass Publics, Political Elites, and McCarthyism[14]

Giving a speech in Wheeling, West Virginia, in 1950 to the Ohio County Women's Republican Club, Senator Joseph McCarthy brayed, "The reason why we find ourselves in a position of impotency . . . is because of the traitorous actions of those . . . who have had all the benefits that the wealthiest nation on earth has had to offer [including] the finest jobs in Government we can give."[15] Waving a document, McCarthy announced, "While I cannot take the time to name all of the men in the State Department who have been named as members of the Communist Party and members of a spy ring, I have here in my hand a list of 205 . . . a list of names that were known to the Secretary of State and who nevertheless are still working and shaping the policy of the State Department."[16]

There were communist spies. There were no spies on McCarthy's list, however, since he had no list of names. This did not prove a problem for him. His sensational charges further fueled his meteoric rise to national fame. For the next four years, he wreaked havoc, destroying the careers and lives of diplomats, scientists, librarians, school teachers, journalists, and on and on—with wild, alcoholically fueled accusations of treason and subversion.[17]

McCarthy's power to ravage the lives of individuals and to deform democratic institutions had two major sources, one noted then and subsequently, the other neglected then and subsequently. The one noted all the time is the power of his mass appeal. McCarthy drove headline story after headline story of treason and betrayal. His capacity to incite—and exploit—public hysteria over communist subversion gave him power. He cowed Washington by campaigning against and crushing senators in the 1950 and 1952 elections who stood up against him. McCarthy could run roughshod over the rights of those he bullied and slandered and ruined because the mass of citizens supported his crusade to root out communists and internal subversion "even if some innocent people should be hurt."[18]

McCarthy's capacity to sway elections is the commonly remarked source of his power to destroy. A second source of his power, tellingly, is rarely remarked. It is party government. Republican control of the United States Senate was the necessary condition of McCarthy being appointed chair of a Senate subcommittee. Without control of a subcommittee, he would never have commanded the institutional resources to wreak destruction on the scale that he did. True, some of the Republican leadership was wary of McCarthy, appointing him chair of the Senate Committee on Government Operations in the belief that it would be a backwater committee. A miscalculation of the first order—and a reminder that the consequences of mistakes by those with power tend to dwarf mistakes by those without power. And McCarthy was hardly being forced down the throat of Republican leaders. On the contrary, Republican leadership stood by him until the end, partly no doubt because of his power to sway voters, but also, for many, out of agreement with his goals and indifference toward or even approval of his methods.[19]

When candidates that McCarthy campaigned against lost, their loss naturally was attributed to his campaigning against them, and taken as evidence of his mass electoral power. I say naturally partly because this was the lesson that experts, including those who despised McCarthy, drew in an effort to understand the spirit of the times, but also because it was the lesson that McCarthy and his sympathizers trumpeted in order to enhance their power. It was a lesson that seemed no more than common sense given the common conviction of the susceptibility of mass publics to demagogues.

There were good reasons at midcentury for this conviction. Hitler's accession to power through free elections was a terrifying example of the power of mass propaganda. Nor could the susceptibility of mass electorates to demagogues be dismissed as a foreign failing. Huey Long was a homegrown example of the gullibility of mass electorates. If the fears of mass irrationality turned out to be ill founded, they were not obviously ill founded. The politics of the 1950s deserved the epithet "the paranoid style."[20]

The claim of mass susceptibility to McCarthy's demagogic style was first challenged by Polsby. One of the scalps McCarthy claimed to have taken—and was universally credited with having taken—was Senator William Benton's. But analyzing Connecticut results, Polsby observed that 1950 was a bad election cycle for Democrats generally, and that Benton, a Democrat, had won the previous election by only a hair.[21] Extending Polsby's initial work, Berinsky and Lenz conducted a comprehensive analysis of county-level results in the 1948–1964 Senate elections.[22] To assess the counterfactual of election outcomes but for McCarthy's intervention, they estimate a model taking account of, among other things, country and state fixed effects; short-term partisan swings (indexed by presidential popularity and the state of the national economy); incumbency (elected or appointed); and challenger quality. The results of their analysis eviscerate the taken-for-granted presumption of McCarthy's electoral power, showing that, to the extent his intervention made any difference at all, it most likely backfired as often as it succeeded. They conclude, "Our analysis suggests that McCarthy's electoral power was illusionary."[23]

One can object that it is easier to get things right in hindsight, and there is truth to this. What is no less striking, however, is the consensus of experts for decades after the 1950s. The lesson of McCarthyism, it was agreed, is the irrationality of mass politics. Between their ignorance and their fears, ordinary citizens are all too susceptible to demagogues. Mass politics are the politics of emotion and pseudo-rationality. In Mencken's dismissive epigram, "Democracy is the art and science of running the circus from the monkey cage."

One lesson of the reanalysis of McCarthyism, however, is that there is markedly more coherence and rootedness to citizens' preferences than Mencken's metaphor allows — sometimes for the better. Just because he was a Republican, McCarthy had an easier time winning the votes of Republicans, but for the same reason, a harder time winning Democratic ones. A second, deeper lesson is that the major source of McCarthy's power was political elites' unfounded fear of mass politics.[24] It is a mistake to minimize the ignorance and gullibility and irrationality of many citizens. It is a bigger mistake, Berinsky and Lenz's results suggest, to neglect the consequences of elites' fears that ordinary citizens are easy pickings for demagogues.

Trust in Government and the Abuse of Authority[25]

It is one thing to argue that mass publics are less of a danger to a democratic politics because they are less easily swayed by demagogues than has been supposed. But it is necessary to go beyond this. Mass publics are not only less of a liability than has been supposed but more of a positive benefit than has been recognized. They provide a check on the abuse of democratic authority.

The standard normative narrative, I recognize, runs in the opposite direction. It is by failing to confide in authority that citizens put a democratic politics at risk. A textbook example: the politics of the 1960s and 1970s. A democratic government, the argument runs, does not have the capacity to extract the degree of compliance necessary for a policy to succeed by force, and it would in any case lose its claim to democratic legitimacy to do so by threats of force. It must count on the readiness of citizens to trust its intentions and competence to secure the compliance necessary for policies to succeed. It must count in the largest measure on voluntary compliance. Governments, when their trustworthiness is called into question, have less of a reservoir of readiness for voluntary compliance to draw on. It follows that, so far as a policy requires the voluntary compliance to succeed, the lower their level of trust in government, the greater the risk of it failing. In turn, the more experience that citizens have of policies failing, the lower the level of trust that they will have in government and the lower their willingness to voluntarily comply. A vicious cycle gets under way: less trust, less voluntary compliance; less voluntary compliance, more failure; more failure, less trust. Slowly at first, then with increasing rapidity, a loss of trust in government undermines governance. "Under-lying discontent is the necessary result, and the potential for revolutionary alteration of the political and social system is enhanced."[26] Hence anxious charting of levels of trust in government.

At the limit, this argument must be right. But it illustrates the costs of considering only the risks of mass politics and neglecting those of elite politics. Consider the last period of massive disorder and protest in American politics, the mid-1960s through the mid-1970s. Popular and scholarly concern was with the hemorrhaging of trust in government, with a loss of confidence in the future of America. Carter's ill-fated "crisis of confidence" came to symbolize the presumption that the root problem was not with the American government but with the American people. It is, I believe, closer to the mark to say that it was the other way around.

Two presidents of the United States were especially culpable. The first, Lyndon Johnson, campaigned in 1964 as the candidate of peace, portraying Goldwater as the candidate of war. Once elected, Johnson, progressively committed more than a half million American soldiers to a bloody and futile war in Vietnam without benefit of a declaration of war. He did so believing: "I don't see what we can ever hope to get out of there with, once we're committed . . . don't think it's worth fighting for and I don't think that we can get out."[27] The response: massive antiwar protests and mini guerilla groups (e.g., the Weathermen). Yes, the protests were disruptive and some deadly. And yes, there was a broad and steep loss of trust in government.[28] But the disorder and distemper were integral to checking the abuse of authority and overcoming a grotesque policy.

Then there is Nixon. Nixon used the powers of the presidency to break the law to increase his chances of winning office before Watergate and retaining it after Watergate. Consider his position when the scandal broke. He knew that he must hold on to public support to survive. He would use all means he believed necessary to do so, including breaking the law.[29] What was his greatest potential asset? Trust in government: The readier citizens are to put their faith in authority, the greater the risk that they are over-ready to yield to authorities. So under the shadow of Watergate, citizens with the most positive views of government were the most supportive of censorship and wiretapping, and the most likely to agree that "Americans should be willing to defend what their country does, even if they feel it has done something wrong."[30] Most strikingly, it is those who trust government the most who are most ready to agree, "There are times when it is necessary for the government to bend or even break the law if it is to do its job."[31] Trust puts democratic government at greater risk than distrust.

This claim can be put in two ways, one negative, the other positive. The negative is that a readiness to resist authority is a necessary break on its abuse. This, I acknowledge, has the same properties as the claim that trust in government is necessary: validity at the limit and vagueness pretty much everywhere else. Under just what conditions is resistance to democratic authority a net benefit? It is, even so, worth considering that the fear of the politically influential—the likelihood that some number of them will go off the rails compounded by the threat to a democratic politics when they do—should be as great, or even greater, than the fear of mass politics. The positive claim is that a challenge to authority is a spur to the dynamics of the democratic idea. Dahl captured this idea, remarking: "For every system purporting to be democratic is vulnerable to the charge that it is not democratic enough, or not 'really' or 'fully' democratic. The charge is bound to be correct since no polity has ever been fully democratized."[32]

No law of history guarantees that liberal democracies will become ever more fully or truly democratic. A democratic politics, just so far as it gives people opportunities to choose, is inherently a risky venture. Voters unavoidably will make bad choices. But it is a nice irony that tough-mindedness in political analysis has consisted in presuming that the guardians of the democratic creed are those who pose the gravest threat to civil liberties—namely, those with political power in their hands. When they go off the rails, as inevitably they will, the challenge to authority by a portion of the public is a part of the remedy.

The Bottom-Up Struggle for Racial Equality[33]

My emphasis has been on the role of parties in circumscribing and yoking together the alternatives on offer. There is a double risk in this emphasis. The narrow one is to slight the role of parties in motivating their supporters to take sides on the choices on offer. The broader risk is to give the impression that the dynamics of mass politics are entirely a top-down organization of the alternatives on offer. A new perspective on the long-run politics of race brings out the bottom-up pressures for change.

In a magisterial study of the American party system and the politics of race, Schickler brings into view for the first time the politics of the "long" civil rights movement.[34] The narrative begins in the 1930s and 1940s. It is a complex story of multiple institutions and processes, including the drive of the Congress of Industrial Organizations (CIO) to organize African Americans and to press the Democratic Party to commit itself to the struggle for civil rights. Of the many idea threads in this account, one in particular spotlights a major limitation in the institutional perspective that I have set out.

It has to do with the conjoining of policy agendas. The commitment of the Republican Party to economic conservatism and of the Democratic Party to economic liberalism arguably dates back to the nineteenth century. Historically, however, the commitment of the Republican Party was to racial liberalism and of the Democratic to racial conservatism. Subsequently, economic and racial policy agendas became aligned. The Republican Party is the party of both economic and racial conservatism, the Democratic Party the party of both economic and racial liberalism.

A keystone question, then, is how racial liberalism became conjoined with economic liberalism, racial conservatism with economic conservatism. My emphasis has been on top-down coupling of policy agendas. Schickler brings out bottom-up pressure. Northern Democratic whites were not the first to tie economic and racial liberalism together, but they were among the first to do so. Northern whites, Schickler shows, connected economic and racial liberalism in both their ideas and actions at the ballot box as early as the late 1930s—well before the national climate of opinion had changed. This discovery offers an account of bottom-up pressure by a faction within the mass public, exerting influence through the medium of a political party, to qualitatively enlarge the American under-standing of equality.

It is not obvious, to me at any rate, how to tie together in any degree of detail bottom-up pressures and top-down co-ordination. But there is a cautionary moral to draw, I believe. The study of the electoral politics of race has concentrated on opposition to policies intended to promote racial equality. It has emphasized the power of prejudice, for good reason. It has questioned whether conservative opposition is grounded in conservatism, with less justification. But in both respects, it has reinforced the one-sided appraisal of mass politics as a potential threat to democratic values and institutions. The hitch is that viewing the public as though it is homogeneous ignores the political cleavages within it and hence the extent to which its ideological wings can contribute to a democratic politics.

CAVEAT LECTOR

Everything has a cost and that includes a chunk of the public being better able to do what so many have wished that citizens could do but have concluded that they cannot—namely, en-gage politics on an ideological basis.

Ideological Polarization

A signal fact of contemporary American politics is the discon-nect between politicians and voters: the positions of Demo-cratic and Republican candidates have become more extreme, but on the best evidence, the positions of voters have not.[35] This disconnect generates dilemmas of rationality.

Voters choose rationally when they choose the alternative closest to their ideal point. Suppose, then, that a moderately liberal Democratic voter has a choice between an extremely liberal Democratic candidate and a moderately conservative Republican. Figure 4.1 depicts this choice situation.

If all that counts are candidates' policy preferences, the Republican candidate is the Democratic voter's rational choice. But what counts more for policy outcomes all in all is which party wins control of government. A moderate Democrat who votes for a moderate Republican candidate casts a vote in support of the Republican Party being the party that controls government.[36] The Democratic voter then would have chosen the alternative that is worse considering her preferences all in all. And the more ideologically polarized the parties, the more self-defeating her vote.

There is an unhappy corollary. Imagine that the American party system enters an ideologically polarized era (that is to say, as it is now). Both parties have become ideologically more homogeneous at the elite level. A moderate Democrat must vote for the candidate of her party, provided only that he lines up to the left of the Republican candidate, however extreme his position.[37] Similarly, a moderate Republican must vote for the candidate of his party, provided only that she lines up to the right of the Democratic candidate, however extreme her position. The outcome is somewhere between paradox and irony. In an ideologically polarized era, partisans who are in ideological synch with their parties but moderate in their views are at risk of making themselves worse off by doing what

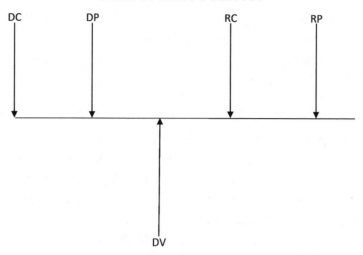

Figure 4.1. Party-centered vs. candidate-centered choice. DV
represents the position of a moderately liberal Democratic voter;
DC the position of an extremely liberal Democratic candidate;
DP the position of the Democratic Party; RC the position of
a moderately conservative Republican candidate; and RP
the position of the Republican Party.

should make them better off—voting rationally. Considering
their preferences all in all, they should vote for the candidate
of their party. There is no logical necessity that the candidate take extreme positions. She may do so or she may not.[38]
But either way, moderate supporters of a party who broadly
agree with their party's outlook—the very model of a modern
ideal citizen, as Gilbert and Sullivan might say—are rationally
obliged to support their candidate. In an ideologically polarized era, moderates in synch with their party are boxed in and
in one sense must vote against themselves. The choices they
must make are between the extremes, but the fact that they

make choices of one or the other extreme does not mean that they value being moderates any the less.

That is one irony. A second irony is that bias is a precondition of good judgment.

A Paradox: Good Judgment and Partisan Bias

Partisans identify emotionally with their party. Their emotions color, it is agreed, their perception and evaluation of issues and events and candidates. In the classic formulation of *The American Voter*, "Identification with a party raises a perceptual screen through which the individual tends to see what is favorable to his partisan orientation. The stronger the party bond, the more exaggerated the process of selection and perception distortion will be."[39] Party identification is a "perceptual screen," to be sure, not a blindfold. Partisans are not unresponsive to reality. But they are disposed to see it in a light favorable to their party. Hence the term "partisan bias."

Bias is a synonym for prejudice. Thus, depending on whether their party might be held responsible or not, Democrats and Republicans are disposed to see unemployment to be increasing or decreasing; inflation worsening or improving; the budget deficit ballooning or shrinking.[40] Results like these are robust. But what, exactly, to make of them is not as obvious as one would like. The budget deficit is a matter of fact. So, too, are unemployment statistics. But it is hard to imagine a discussion at the family dinner table where the numbers of either are explicitly discussed. Things better or worse, yes, but anecdotally or broad brush: discussion does— and Aristotle might add should—proceed with the precision appropriate to its purpose.

Which applies, with a force that I do not believe has been properly appreciated, to public opinion interviews. Respondents are taught, by taking part in a survey on political issues, how to respond. Time is the big constraint. So the objective of investigators is to ask as many questions as can be clearly put to respondents within the amount of time they have. The result is to teach respondents a practice of speedy responses. It is not, to be clear, that respondents are encouraged to respond thoughtlessly; it is that they are trained to respond straightaway.

For the measurement of some attributes, immediate responses are just what is in order. But not for the measurement of political knowledge, as a set of strikingly innovative studies demonstrates—strikingly because the innovations are so simple. Thus, Prior, Sood, and Khanna showed a marked increase in correct responses to knowledge about politics questions by providing modest financial incentives to get things right and by appealing to respondents to respond as accurately as they were able.[41] The findings of Bullock and his colleagues are still more directly on target. They show that a modest incentive substantially reduces the extent to which Democrats and Republicans part company about the facts of the matter. Moreover, their results show that incentives to acknowledge that one does not know the right answer virtually eliminates partisan bias.[42]

Still, it must be conceded that the question at issue is not just whether citizens know or fail to know the facts of the matter. Breaking new ground, Gaines and his colleagues contrast interpreting versus knowing the facts. They show that Republicans and Democrats were equally well informed about the facts of the second Iraq War—for example, casualty levels. But they interpreted the facts differently. Thus, strong Democrats most often categorized casualty levels as "large or very large," strong Republicans as "moderate."[43]

How, then, should we think of partisan bias? What type of reasoning is it? In a celebrated formulation, Kunda distinguished reasoning motivated by a desire for accuracy from reasoning motivated by a desire "to arrive at a particular conclusion," or to use the term of art, "motivated directional biases."[44] Partisan bias, it would seem, is a paradigmatic example of a motivated directional bias. Lodge and Taber display partisan bias as the centerfold illustration of their general theory of political "reasoning." The reasoning of partisans, they declare, is driven by "partisan goals, which motivate them to apply their reasoning powers in defense of a prior, specific conclusion."[45] Partisan reasoning, on this reasoning, is inherently distorted reasoning. Strong partisans, far from undertaking an "evenhanded treatment of policy arguments," find it impossible to be fair-minded.[46]

The tipoff that there is certainly a puzzle, and possibly a paradox, is Lodge and Taber's discovery that it is the most politically knowledgeable, the most politically sophisticated, who are the most likely to engage in motivated political reasoning. They are the most likely to direct their attention to arguments that confirm what they already believe; to spend time and energy picking holes in arguments at odds with their beliefs; and, given the opportunity, to focus on information that supports what they already believe.

There is something curious about a claim that the most politically knowledgeable and sophisticated are the people whose reasoning is most likely to be distorted to show that what they already believe is right, is right. To say that this claim is curious is not to assert that it is empirically wrong, still less to contend that it is logically incoherent. It is to say that the conclusion to draw from the claim may be a surprising one. So it is here.

The normative standard of rational updating is Bayesian reasoning.[47] It seems straightforwardly to follow that, if two partisans—say, a strong Democrat and a strong Republican—take account of new information in accordance with the Bayesian ideal, over time their views will converge. Bullock, however, has demonstrated that, on the contrary, they will overcome their disagreement, but only if they "receive political messages so numerous and so credible that their prior beliefs are overwhelmed."[48] Need it be said that this is a rare state of affairs in the real world of politics? The persistence of partisan disagreement, it follows, is not evidence in itself of a desire "to arrive at a particular conclusion." Just so far as partisans understand that parties stand for different views about both what ought to be done and how what ought to be done ought to be done, they have rational grounds for disagreement about issues that the parties do contest. They know and agree with what their party broadly stands for; they know and disagree with what the other party broadly stands for. Now comes a moment where they must make a choice, say, to support or oppose Obamacare. What can it possibly mean to say that programmatically committed Democrats and Republicans should give "evenhanded treatment of policy arguments"?[49] Both sides, given their beliefs and values, have good reason to have confidence in some lines of argument, skepticism about others. It would be irrational for either to proceed otherwise.

How does this cash out? Electoral competition through the medium of political parties, a necessary condition of a democratic politics, ensures that there is no God's-eye view of live issues. Disagreement is the point of a democratic politics.

Epilogue

REALISM

IF one were looking for a slogan to sum up the all-in-all argument I have been making, one possibility is, ideas matter in politics, even, odd as it may sound, in mass politics. Yes, it is routinely conceded that a portion of the public has put together an ideologically coherent view of politics. But it simultaneously is insisted that this portion is distinguished precisely by its size, namely, inconsiderable. The principal thing to know, it is standardly agreed, is that citizens pay attention to politics and public affairs only fitfully; think about them only sporadically; and know or care little about them.

Skepticism is the lesson. But skepticism comes in degrees. Achen and Bartels's *Democracy for Realists* is uncompromising. Their argument has many strands, and it is certainly fair to say that some of them are provocative.[1] My own interest is a narrow one, public opinion and political ideology.[2] Their views on public opinion are mainstream. Because they are so well put and delivered with such force, their work makes plain how much is at stake.

Realism is their battle cry.[3] The real world is as it is; real people are as they are; and we need to be tough-minded enough to face up to that reality. A good motto for science but in their usage a paradoxical one. Political realism standardly entails a readiness to look behind avowed intentions to the actual motives of self interest and group interest. Realism so understood has been a standard model of democratic politics since *The Federalist*. Groups compete or cooperate, whichever they calculate is to their advantage. Their objective is to be better off, where better off usually means economically better off.

Groups are the basis of politics for Achen and Bartels, too. But their realism is of a novel form. It is the opposite of realistic conflict. It is an autopsy of the pathologies of citizens' calculations of what is to their advantage.[4] It is not that voters are not concerned about what is in their interest. It is that they are inept at doing so. They make many mistakes. Many of their mistakes are silly. Worse, they don't learn from their mistakes. They make the same ones time after time.

But this is not surprising from Achen and Bartels's perspective. For them, group politics is not about interests but about identities. It is the answer to the question, who am I?—or rather the many answers a person may give: Catholic in response to the first Catholic candidate for president of the United States; Southern and white in response to a perceived assault on the folkways of the South. By way of illustration, Achen and Bartels present summary examples of identity politics—the Boston Irish in the 1920s and 1930s; Catholics and Protestants in the 1960 election; race and realignment in the South; among others.[5]

What, then, is their foundational basis for a theory of mass politics? Social psychology in the form of Social Identity Theory. Their account of Social Identity Theory is elliptical. It is not entirely clear whether they are advocating the technical theory of social identity—or more exactly, self-categorization—or a commonsense version of it.[6] What is clear is that their psychological emphasis shines a spotlight on a possible Achilles' heel of the account of ideological partisans that I have set out.

Partisans with a politically coherent outlook are not the exception nowadays. They are commonplace. That is a result that I have reported and emphasized. Achen and Bartels accept this result. So they remark, "A party constructs a *conceptual viewpoint* by which its voters can make sense of the political world. Sympathetic newspapers, magazines, websites, and television channels convey the framework to partisans. That framework identifies friends and enemies, it supplies talking points, and it tells people how to think and what to believe. . . . For voters who identify with a party, partisanship *pulls together conceptually* nearly every aspect of politics."[7]

A large bloc of party identifiers, we have seen, engage politics on an ideological basis: the positions they take on the primary policy agendas, their conception of their overall political outlook, their sense of what the party they identify with stands for—all speak to a coherent encompassing outlook on politics, conservative if Republican, liberal if Democrat. But Achen and Bartels are sure that this pattern of beliefs and convictions and political points of view means the opposite of what I take it to mean.

Partisanship "pull[ing] together" one's view of the

world—that is the key for Achen and Bartels. An emotional attachment to a party comes first, positions on issues after and as a product of the emotional attachment to a party. As they put it, "the political preferences and judgments that look and feel like the bases of partisanship and voting behavior are, in reality, often *consequences* of party and group loyalties."[8] We may believe that we reasoned our way to our positions on issues; we may even be able to give reasons for them. But we had the beliefs before we had the reasons to have the beliefs. And we have the beliefs that we do because we have the emotional attachments that we do. To borrow their chapter title, "It Feels Like We're Thinking: The Rationalizing Voter." And if voters are not thinking but instead rationalizing their feelings, what sense does it make to speak of their engaging politics on an ideological basis whether or not they make ideologically consistent choices?

Achen and Bartels are right to underline that people typically identify with a party before acquiring a point of view on politics. But the issue is not whether they first identify with a party, and then acquire a perspective on politics. It is not even whether they first identify with a party, and then, as a consequence of identifying with a party, acquire a perspective on politics. The issue is the causal process connecting party identification and political perspectives.

That process is rationalization, Achen and Bartels contend. Rationalization is a logical possibility. But Achen and Bartels present no evidence that it is the one at work. And logically possible is not at all the same as psychologically plausible. Rationalization means justification. To whom do partisans feel a need to justify identifying with a political party?

Not to themselves. There is no evidence that ordinary citizens who identify with a party are troubled by having an emotional attachment to it and, in consequence, feel a need to explain to themselves why they support one party rather than the other. Nor is there evidence or reason to believe that they feel a need to justify it to others. And, even if they did feel a need to justify identifying with a party, whether to themselves or to others, why would they feel it necessary to adopt a whole idea system, to work through the connections between their partisanship, their broad outlook on politics, their understanding of the ideological logic of the party system, and their position on issue after issue? Why wouldn't adopting a position on this or that issue do the trick?

If not rationalization, then what might be the process connecting partisanship and political perspectives? An obvious possibility is learning. Becoming a supporter of a party can help motivate people to learn the causes that it supports and those it opposes. Not every party identifier is motivated to learn about the ideas that her party stands for, of course; but the better informed about politics, the more deeply engaged they are, the more likely they are to have internalized the political point of view that their party represents. Achen and Bartels are well aware that this is so. Indeed, they believe that it is a point in their favor, remarking that "the more information the voter has, often the better able she is to bolster her identities with rational-sounding reasons."[9]

This is a curious conjecture. It amounts to asserting that those who are the best at thinking—that is, the best informed about politics—are the ones who are most likely to only think that they're thinking. It is surely simpler, and more plausible, to suppose that the best informed are the best at making the connections between the party that they identify with, their conception of their overall outlook on politics, and the positions that they take because they have learned the most about politics. In any case, a perspective on politics, once acquired, whatever the reason it was acquired, is directive. A person may become liberal (or conservative) in politics because of a childhood trauma, or a deep feature of their personality, or socialization in college, or their identification and involvement with a political party: whatever the originating factor, just so far as she is liberal (or conservative), she will take the liberal (or conservative) side of issues.

Ideas matter because they direct choices. To suppose that the political ideas are rationalizations of feelings and no more is to miss what a large part of democratic politics is about.

DISAGREEMENT

Political parties present electorates with systematically divergent alternatives in part because a large number of their supporters are capable of doing what public opinion analysts contend that they are incapable of doing—namely, engaging politics on an ideological basis. This is far from an unmixed blessing. Ideological coherence reinforces legislative gridlock.[10] It contributes to the polarization of contemporary American politics.[11] It locks moderate partisans into supporting their party. In the process, it opens the door for candidates of their party to move to the extreme poles of politics.[12]

No doubt, this is not the full price of a swath of citizens engaging politics on an ideological basis. Yet, it is because they are capable of doing so that a democratic politics can operate full out. For disagreement over ends and means—systematic, insistent, institutionalized disagreement—makes a democratic politics go. It is what checks authority, clarifies alternatives, drives change, enlarges understanding of one's own views and others', promotes tolerance (when more civil than otherwise), reduces the vulnerability of citizens to manipulation by elites, and all in all spurs a democratic politics to become more truly, more fully democratic.[13] It is not that disagreement suffices; that any choice is as good as any other. It is that, when choices are made in a democratic politics, there is no way to get a God's-eye view of what is at stake; no way, in Bernard Williams's pithy phrase, to take the politics out of the choices.[14]

Is it necessary to add that sometimes the wrong choice is made? There are reasons to have faith in a democratic politics. Ultimately, however, it is a matter of faith.

THE 2016 PRESIDENTIAL ELECTION

How does the outcome of the 2016 election square with the arguments that I have made? A fair question. Writing in the immediate aftermath, I am in no position to give a confident, still less a complete, answer. But a few comments in the margin suggest themselves.

The push of prejudice to the Republican candidate was striking, and the results in Chapter 3 provide a foretaste of properly comprehensive analyses of the profit that Donald Trump pocketed from racism. No less striking, though, was the absence of a pull toward the Democratic candidate. Her most explicit focus was narrow: women and minorities, the so-called Brown-is-the-new-White strategy. Not a winning strategy, as it turned out. Candidates forfeit support they don't attempt to win.

Forfeit whose support? The "white working class," in the newly fashionable phrase. A curious phrase since it racializes a strategy the point of which is to make a universalistic appeal.

The power of universalistic appeals to trump particularistic ones was one of the deeper lessons of the civil rights movement. At its peak, it won the support of white Americans by the force of morally universalistic arguments. The crusade for racial equality was not propelled solely by morally universalistic arguments, of course. The injustices done to blacks gave a living force to the crusade for wide public support. But with success the terms of argument narrowed. Appeals for public support that had been made on morally universalistic grounds were made on racially particularistic ones. But just so far as the arguments against injustice were tied to the wrongs done to a particular group, they were morally particularistic. They did not for that reason lack force. But they were not the strongest possible. More support can be won for government to help those in need of help if the effort is made in behalf of all and not just some in need. That was the hypothesis my colleagues and I put to a test.

We conducted a series of experiments. Some experiments varied why there should be job training programs for blacks out of work, because of the historic injustices that have been done to them or because there ought to be such programs for those out of work regardless of race. Other experiments varied both whether the justification as well as the beneficiaries of a policy are racially particularistic or universalistic. The results were striking. Majorities can be won for liberal policies that attract only a minority when they are racially particularistic, by making the policies inclusive and arguing for them on morally universalistic grounds.[15] There is, we concluded, a winning coalition on issues of inequality, very much including racial inequality—provided policies are genuinely inclusive.

That was true when we conducted these studies.[16] That is true now.

Appendix: Summary of Replication

Replication was conducted on Stata-format data files from the ANES 1987 Pilot Study.[1] All variable coding and interpretation is based on codebooks found there.[2]

The data consists of 457 observations of individuals who were interviewed according to two questionnaires (Form A, in which individuals were asked their views on policy and then their [retrospective] thoughts on the topic, and Form B, in which individuals were asked to stop and provide their views on a policy before being asked their view) in two waves.

SAMPLE RESTRICTIONS

Sample sizes from Table 1.2 were approximately replicated by dropping all individuals who answered "Haven't thought much about this," "Don't know," or "N/A" to relevant policy questions in either Wave 1 or Wave 2.

QUESTIONS

For "Stop and Think" questions, variables for eight "Mentions" (in two groups of four) were found and included for questions on Jobs and Government Services; twelve "Mentions" (three groups of four) were found and included for Aid to Blacks. In addition, thoughts (up to three) associated with the respondent's answer to direct inquiries about support for the policy (coded as [Question number]-PF10[letter] in the codebook) were also included.

For "retrospective" questions, two groups of responses were included: (1) the four "Mentions" immediately provided prior to guided prompts, and (2) (up to three) thoughts associated with the respondent's answer to the direct inquiry into his or her position on the policy. Guided/directed prompts that followed the initial four mentions were excluded.[3]

FORMS

Form assignments were accomplished using Wave 1 responses—those responding to "retrospective" questions were assigned Form A and those responding to "stop and think" prompts Form B. Almost all individuals appeared to receive the same form for Wave 2 as Wave 1, with the exception of two respondents who answered questions on Government Services in Wave 2 from the wrong form, and four who answered questions on Black Aid in Wave 2 from the wrong form. Sample sizes were best matched by leaving these individuals associated with their Wave 1 form.

CODING RESPONSES

The number of thoughts that were *liberal*, *conservative*, or *ambiguous* was calculated by summing the number of thoughts that were given "Direction Codes" of 1 ("Favors liberal side of issue"), 2 ("Favors conservative side of issue"), or 3 ("Mention indicates ambivalence, conflict"), respectively, for each policy question across both waves for each individual. The number of *star codes* is the sum of the number of thoughts across both waves for which the "Content Code" was 122, 123, 124, 129, 145, 243, 244, 245, 313.[4]

Conflicting Consideration Counts: Conflicting consideration counts were calculated as the minimum of the number of *liberal* and *conservative* thoughts.

Spontaneous statements of ambivalence or conflict: Ambivalence thought counts were calculated as the number of thoughts coded as *ambiguous*.

Two-sided remarks (star codes): Star-code remarks were calculated as the number of thoughts with content codes 122, 123, 124, 129, 145, 243, 244, 245, 313.

Table A.1 Reproduction of conflicting considerations results

Conflicts	Retrospective			Stop and Think		
	Jobs	Services	Blacks	Jobs	Services	Blacks
0	73.9 (%)	57.8	73.4	36.9	30.7	29
1	22.6	33.6	22.6	27.3	25	21.6
2	3.5	5.2	4	22.2	21.6	25
3+	0.0	3.4	0.0	13.1	18.7	24.4
Ambivalence						
0	77	83	79	63	72	71
1+	23	17	21	37	28	29
Two-sided						
0	86	94	81	73	93	72
1+	14	6	19	27	7	28
Sample size	108	109	118	173	168	165

Source: Reproduced from Zaller and Feldman 1992, p. 592, Table 2.

Table A.2 Replication of conflicting considerations results

Conflicts	Retrospective			Stop and Think		
	Jobs	Services	Blacks	Jobs	Services	Blacks
0	79 (%)	61	77	37	32	30
1	18	30	19	28	29	22
2	4	5	3	22	21	24
3+	0	4	0	13	18	24
Sample size	108	109	118	173	168	165

Notes

PROLOGUE

1. Sniderman and Carmines 1997.
2. Sniderman and Stiglitz 2008.
3. This is a joint line of research with Edward G. Carmines.

CHAPTER I. PREFERENCE REVERSALS

1. Zaller 1992, p. 76. This is not a stray claim or slip of the pen. The charge is repeated, with still more gusto: According to Zaller, most of the people, most of the time, just "make it up as they go along"— "Making It Up as You Go Along" is the title of Chapter 5 in Zaller 1992.

2. For the most uncompromising presentation of this position, see Bartels 2003.

3. Preference reversals strictly defined are violations of rationality canonically defined. See Kahneman 2011, pp. 354–362. For the distinction between equivalence and emphasis conceptions of framing, see Druckman 2001. An unremarked irony is that strict framing effects— e.g., weighting losses over gains—are demonstrations of response invariance. More fundamentally, the reinterpretation of framing effects that I offer applies to framing broadly, not strictly, defined.

4. Zaller 1992, p. 76.
5. Achen 1975, p. 122.
6. Bartels 2003, p. 51; italics mine.

7. Converse 1964.

8. Zaller and Feldman 1992.

9. Bartels 2013, p. 472.

10. Picking as an example a hot-button issue like race may seem a rhetorical ploy. In fact, it is one of the policy issues that Zaller and Feldman 1992 specifically offer as evidence in support of their theory.

11. For that matter, it is a form of conceptual extravagance to invoke a whole new set of causal agents, the so-called considerations. Though they are meant to provide a routine explanation of survey responses, evidence of them can be produced only by requiring respondents to do what they ordinarily do not do in public opinion surveys, a point I discuss later. And if the bloating of causal explanations by the insertion of unobservables were not sufficient liabilities, I cannot see a way to settle the causal order—are considerations the reasons for people taking an issue position, or are they justifications for having taken one? See, for example, McGraw, Lodge, and Stroh 1990 and Lodge and Taber 2013. See also Zaller's acknowledgment of the problem of causal order and his response. Zaller 1992, p. 64, n. 13.

12. Zaller and Feldman 1992, p. 585.

13. The Random House Unabridged English Dictionary, s.v. "ambivalence"; italics mine.

14. Zaller and Feldman's 1992 estimates of ambivalence are the sum of "considerations" pro and con in two interviews, seven months apart.

15. Zaller and Feldman 1992, p. 609.

16. Zaller and Feldman 1992, p. 586.

17. Zaller and Feldman 1992, p. 586.

18. Zaller and Feldman 1992, p. 579.

19. Zaller 1992 is insistent on this claim, asserting that "most people, on most issues, do not 'really think' any particular thing," p. 194; "most people really aren't sure what their opinions are on most political matters," p. 76; indeed, that most of the people, most of the time, just "make it up as they go along" (see n. 1).

20. Zaller and Feldman 1992, p. 612.

21. The decision rule is to average pro and con considerations: under this rule, discrete responses that are simultaneously pro and con score zero.

22. Zaller went above and beyond any reasonable expectation in as-

sisting the replication. I am deeply indebted to him. Table A.1, is a copy of the original results; Table A.2 the replication of them. Though not identical, the replication results and the original results are strikingly similar. I invite close comparison of the two.

23. Yes, I am aware that Zaller and Feldman 1992 sum responses over their three different measures to accumulate a substantial number of "ambivalents." But this is not reasonable, partly because the other conceptions of ambivalence are not relevant to their theory; additionally, because the increase in numbers of the ambivalent is testimony that the measures are measuring things different from one another.

24. Taking the government services issue as an example, respondents are first asked, "Could you tell me what kinds of things come to mind when you think about cutting government services?"; then, *separately*, they are asked, "What kinds of things come to mind when you think about increases in government services?" Zaller and Feldman 1992, p. 587.

25. Lodge and Taber 2013, p. 214; italics in original.

26. "Individuals at the simple end of the complexity continuum tend to rely on fixed, one-dimensional evaluative rules in interpreting events and to make decisions on the basis of only a few salient items of information. Individuals at the complex end tend to interpret events in multidimensional terms and to integrate a variety of evidence in making decisions." Tetlock 1984, p. 366.

27. Zaller and Feldman 1992, p. 589; italics in original.

28. It would appear that the pairing rule also contradicts Zaller and Feldman's Axiom 2, which holds that individuals answer survey questions by averaging across salient considerations at the time of choice. Zaller and Feldman 1992, p. 586. Two people cannot be equally likely, on each occasion, to switch positions over time.

29. Zaller and Feldman 1992, p. 609.

30. Rahn 1993; Jacoby 1988; Kam 2005.

31. Bartels 2003, p. 51; italics mine.

32. Lenz 2012, 2009.

33. Lenz 2009, p. 821. See Lenz 2012 for a full and finely articulated presentation of the argument.

34. Lenz 2009, p. 834.

35. Lenz 2009, p. 831.

36. For the three of the four issues, approximately four in ten knew the parties' positions before the election; for the fourth, only a quarter. See Lenz 2009, Tables 1, 2, 3, and 4.

37. Lenz reports additional results that give weight to a blind-following hypothesis. See Lenz 2009, pp. 206–209.

38. A claim that parties act as reference groups is a more complex—and productive—claim than it may seem at first. Lenz makes an important distinction between "cue following" and "blind following" and shows that, for low-information voters, the latter more aptly fits the results than the former. Lenz 2012, pp. 206–211. There are many parallels between his account and the distinction I will draw between yielding and understanding and the importance of political knowledge, particularly of the ideological structure of the party system.

39. E.g., Rahn 1993; Iyengar and Valentino 2000.

40. Bullock 2011. Bullock's analysis is exemplary for its clarity and depth.

41. Bullock 2011, p. 496.

42. Slothuus 2010. Absent pre-post data, just when Social Democrats came to the view that the welfare system was under stress is indeterminate. Slothuus addresses this question, albeit indirectly, demonstrating that the three-way interaction between Part Frame × Social Democrat identifiers × Welfare Belief interaction is not statistically significant.

43. See my discussion of party cues and the distinction between yielding and understanding in Chapter 3.

44. Boudreau 2015.

45. This section is based on Sniderman and Theriault 2004.

46. Gamson and Modigliani 1989, p. 3.

47. Gamson and Modigliani 1989, p. 3.

48. Nelson and Kinder 1996, p. 1057. See also Entmann 1993.

49. Nelson, Clawson, and Oxley 1997.

50. One of the many advances that Chong and Druckman have made in the study of framing is to call attention to the importance of the strength of the arguments being made on opposing sides of issues. It is necessary and sufficient, on their approach, to assess the strength of considerations from an impartial perspective. That this is an important step forward is, I believe, clear. That it is a sufficient one, however, is to

assume that there is a God's-eye view of the matter. See, e.g., Chong and Druckman 2007.

51. Grice 1989.

52. For an incisive summary and evaluation of Grice's concept of conversational logic, see Soames 2005.

53. Nelson, Clawson, and Oxley 1997.

54. The rally experiment was carried out in the second Multi-Investigator Survey, 1998–1999. Replication was as close as could be managed using a different mode—telephone interviewing as opposed to laboratory experiment. For a detailed description and presentation of results, see Sniderman and Theriault 2004.

55. Langer, Blank, and Chanowitz 1978.

56. This section draws on Jackman and Sniderman 2006.

57. The distinction between content-laden and content-free is inescapably a matter of degree. A content-free condition cannot be perfectly free of content without being semantically vacuous.

58. The vagueness of "more" sensibly, "more" likely, can be maddening. But matters of degree are inherently muzzy.

CHAPTER 2. AN ECOLOGICAL THEORY
OF IDEOLOGICAL CONSISTENCY

Epigraph: Kinder 2006, p. 199.

1. The argument and analysis builds on the theory of spatial reasoning and party identification that Edward Stiglitz and I have developed (Sniderman and Stiglitz 2012). Stiglitz thus deserves credit for the foundations of the argument and analysis, but not culpability for their extension.

2. It is now commonly accepted that coherence at the level of policy agendas is a feature of public opinion. Carmines and Layman 1997 were leaders in introducing the concept of policy agendas.

3. It does not follow, if you take the position that ordinary citizens are not capable of forming an ideologically grounded belief system, or even that their views on most issues are fuzzy, that you are ruling out preference consistency and policy-grounded voting. See Goren 2013 for an important demonstration of the intermediate role of "policy principles" as organizing mechanisms of choice.

4. Campbell et al. 1960, p. 193.

5. Campbell et al. 1960, p. 193.

6. Converse 1964, p. 211.

7. See Peffley and Hurwitz 1985, also, with respect to whether liberalism and conservatism have more than one dimension. See Conover and Feldman 1981 for exposition of what it means to characterize an ideology as multidimensional. But under all variations, the distinguishing feature of ideological reasoning remains — namely, derivation of specific choices from abstract capstone concepts.

8. Converse 1964, pp. 215-216.

9. Not surprisingly, there is some volatility in the proportions classified as ideologues, partly as a result of differing salience of references to liberal and conservative in election contests, partly on how fine-grained the classifications are. For an analytical review of the relevant research, see Kinder and Kalmoe 2008, 2009, 2010. My references are to Kinder and Kalmoe's APSA papers. They are the only work in the public domain. It was not possible to obtain a copy of their forthcoming book. Fortunately, Achen and Bartels have, with permission to cite and quote. Wherever possible I have chosen assertions cited by Achen and Bartels.

10. "Precious few" is Kinder's term. Kinder 1998, p. 796. For "abstract and far-reaching dimensions," see Converse 1964, pp. 216-217.

11. Respondents who did think the parties differed ideologically were asked a series of follow-up questions, to see if they might nonetheless know what it means to say that one of the parties is more conservative than the other. If they answered yes, they then were asked, "What do you have in mind when you say that the Republicans (Democrats) are more conservative (liberal) than the Democrats (Republicans)?" Follow-up questions were put to respondents to determine what they "had in mind" when they said that the Republican Party was more conservative than the Democratic Party. The largest number, on the order of 60 percent, got the heart of the matter right, identifying the Democratic Party as more supportive of government services and spending; the Republican Party as more committed to holding down government spending. My calculation is based on Table II (Converse 1964, p. 221) — specifically, respondents who satisfied either "recognition and proper matching of label, meaning, and party" and a broad understanding of the terms "conservative" and "liberal" or "recognition and proper matching but a narrow definition of terms (like 'spend-save')." See the legend for

Table III in Converse (1964, p. 224). For many, to be sure, their conception was spare, principally consisting in a distinction between readiness to spend or to save. Then again, the "spend-save" items are the core of Stimson's 2004 primary mood measure, mainly on the basis of whether government spending across an array of social programs should be increased or decreased. Also, see my discussion later in this chapter of the social welfare policy agenda.

12. I owe the term "ecological" and the perspective it summarizes to Gibson 1986. For an independent, parallel argument on prior organization of political choice sets, see Stone and Buttice 2010.

13. But only partly. Others are presented in response to contributors, activists, interest groups, and intense policy demanders of all stripes. No less important, though less explored, other alternatives are not presented at all for the same reason.

14. Snyder and Ting 2002, p. 91.

15. Campbell et al. 1960, p. 193.

16. Luskin 1987, p. 862.

17. These examples are selected from Ellis and Stimson 2012, p. 44, Table 3.2.

18. Tomz and Sniderman 2005.

19. Converse 1964, p. 214.

20. Converse 1964.

21. "General engagement with politics" operationally turns out to be a synonym for factual knowledge of politics; Kinder and Kalmoe 2009. Kinder and Kalmoe sometimes point to cognitive limits, too, contending that having a meaningful understanding of an ideological identity is "largely a matter of interest and ability." Kinder and Kalmoe 2008, p. 12.

22. Kinder and Kalmoe 2009, p. 19.

23. For a generalized theory of changes in party positions, see Karol 2009.

24. Converse 1964, p. 214.

25. I owe the quote to Gauchet 1997, p. 245.

26. See Sniderman and Stiglitz 2012 for the full argument.

27. For parsimony, two conditions, identifying with a party and identifying oneself with the same ideological outlook as one's party, are condensed into one.

28. Carmines and Stimson 1989 is the classic work.

29. The exact number qualifying as knowing the parties' ideological reputations depends, of course, on the precise measure used. On the measure I favor, more qualify than on the one that Converse 1964 employed.

30. See Druckman, Peterson, and Slothuus 2013 for analysis bringing into view for the first time an array of consequences of elite polarization. For reinforcement of aversive reactions to the opposing party, see Iyengar and Westwood 2015.

31. These numbers are based on counting as partisans respondents who identify as strong, weak, or leaning identifiers.

32. 46 percent. ANES 2012.

33. The customary measure of association in this problem area is the Pearson product-moment. Because there is a settled sense of when its magnitude is comparatively small or comparatively large, I use it here. Later in the chapter, analyzing trends, unstandardized regression coefficients are used to take account of potentially misleading differences in variance across groups.

34. All issue measures are scored such that a higher score is a conservative score; so, too, is the measure of ideological identification. A positive coefficient is thus a mark of political consistency.

35. Achen 1982, pp. 60–61.

36. For ideological partisans, the unstandardized coefficients for spending on child care and the environment, for example, are .769 and .552; the equivalent coefficients for government services and government helping with jobs are .630 and .583, respectively.

37. The measure of commitment to traditional values consists of three items: degree of agreement or disagreement with the propositions that the world is changing and we should adjust (reverse scored); that new lifestyles are breaking down society; and that there should be more emphasis on traditional family values.

38. With the exception of independents who know the ideological reputations of the parties—a clue to other conditions under which citizens may have politically coherent preferences.

39. In 2012, just under half of the sample (46 percent) and just over half of party identifiers (53 percent) qualified as ideological partisans.

40. I confess that I was taken aback by the size of the coefficients

for ideological partisans because I, at least, have never before had associations of this magnitude to report in my research.

41. Converse 1964, p. 228, Table VIII.

42. To repeat, the issue matrices in Converse's 1964 and the ANES studies differ in many respects, not least time. Converse's findings are of use only as providing a yardstick of what the linkages in extremely constrained and very weakly constrained belief systems look like.

43. The Index of Political Information consists of four items: knowledge of the secretary of the Treasury, the unemployment rate, the party that came second in House seats won, and the secretary of the United Nations.

44. "Ideologically coherent" and "politically coherent" are not synonyms. Nie, Verba, and Petrocik 1979 made the argument that levels of political coherence, indexed by levels of belief constraint, vary with the extent to which politics is arousing. Their argument took a knock when studies demonstrated that the observed increase in constraint beginning in the mid-1960s was in all probability a product of a change in item format. See Sullivan et al. 1979 and Bishop et al. 1978.

45. See, e.g., Poole and Rosenthal 1997; McCarty, Poole, and Rosenthal 2006.

46. This is debatable. While their ideal points are moving farther apart, this is not actually evidence that absolute positions are more extreme. Essentially, ideal points put people on an arbitrary spectrum such that, under a number of assumptions, the distance between individuals reflects the probability they will vote together. The fact that parties are "moving apart" in the Poole-Rosenthal data only means that voting is more polarized.

47. See Knight 1985. Knight's method of classification is based on the classic measure of levels of conceptualization. Consistent with the established approach, ideological identification and party identification are treated as separate and independent.

48. See Levendusky 2009 for evidence that partisan sorting in the electorate is a response to partisan polarization at the elite level.

49. See especially Levendusky 2009 for the canonical account of this process of alignment of partisanship and ideological identification.

50. For convenience of presentation, I use a measure of issue liberalism-conservatism made up of three indicators that repeatedly ap-

peared in ANES over the years—government assistance for jobs and standard of living, level of government services, and government versus private medical insurance. The government services item was first asked about in 1982.

51. See Achen 1982, pp. 58–61.

52. Campbell et al. 1960, p. 193.

53. Possessing this piece of information appears to be a necessary condition of ideological reasoning, so far as fallible measures can sustain a claim of necessity. Possessing this information also appears to be a sufficient condition, on the understanding that those who know it do not know only it.

54. In the 2012 ANES, just over half of party identifiers are, by the criteria I have identified, ideological partisans.

55. It is a curiosity that the notion of party identification as a social identity enjoys so much wider a currency than party identification as a political identity.

CHAPTER 3. MYRDAL'S INSIGHT

1. See Roberts and Klibanoff 2006 for a gripping account of the struggle of those in the South to win the attention of the national press.

2. Hyman and Sheatsley 1956, 1964; Greeley and Sheatsley 1971; Taylor, Sheatsley, and Greeley 1978.

3. Kinder and Sears 1981, p. 416.

4. O'Gorman 1975; O'Gorman and Garry 1976.

5. The "we" is Thomas Piazza and myself. See Sniderman and Piazza 1993.

6. See Sniderman and Piazza 1993, p. 41.

7. Huddy and Feldman 2009, p. 427.

8. In the 1992 ANES, the correlation was .14; in the 1990 GSS, .09; in the 1991 Race and Politics Study, .13.

9. Sniderman and Carmines 1997; Feldman and Huddy 2005.

10. Sniderman and Carmines 1997, pp. 59–98, Ch. 3, "The Power of Prejudice."

11. Dollard 1957.

12. Myrdal 1944.

13. Myrdal 1944, p. lxxiii; italics in original.

14. Myrdal 1994, p. lxxi; italics in original.

15. In fact, Myrdal explicitly rejected the compliment that he had predicted what was going to happen in American race relations, insisting that *An American Dilemma* was not a "futuristic" work. He did take credit for foreseeing that the late 1940s was a time of change and, more particularly, the "Negro rebellion." See Myrdal 1973, pp. 293–308.

16. Again I commend Roberts and Klibanoff 2006 for an enthralling account of the role of the news media in bringing the drama of the civil rights movement to the attention of a national audience.

17. Among other forms of discrimination, including religious, ethnic, nationality, and gender.

18. Southern 1987.

19. Myrdal 1973.

20. Myrdal 1973, pp. 298 ff.

21. For late capitalism, see, e.g., Khair 2015; for the Protestant ethic, see, e.g., Kinder and Sears 1981.

22. See the afterword, "The Redefined Meanings of the Concepts of Symbolic Racism and Racial Resentment," at the end of this chapter.

23. This section draws on the conceptualization of prejudice that underpins the research of my colleagues and myself. See Sniderman, Peri, De Figuerido, and Piazza 2000, pp. 17–25.

24. The instrument for the National Race and Politics Study was the collective creation of Martin Gilens, Jon Hurwitz, Kathleen Knight, James H. Kuklinski, Mark Peffley, and Laura Stoker as well as Edward G. Carmines and Paul M. Sniderman. For reports on the study, see Peffley and Hurwitz 1998 and Sniderman and Carmines 1997.

25. See Chudy 2015 for an innovative analysis of the role of racial sympathy.

26. See Sherif, Sherif, and Nebergall 1965.

27. Tesler and Sears note the problem of arbitrariness. Tesler and Sears 2010, pp. 170–171, n. 7.

28. The minimal loading for the positive adjectives is .7149; the median loading of negative adjectives is –.2131; the largest loading is –.263.

29. Factor analysis results available on request.

30. Alpha =.89. There is a disposition to proceed as though there are strict boundaries between the cognitive and the affective. This may

possibly be the case in some circumstances, but they are rare. I use the term "evaluations." But, of course, evaluations of blacks as "lazy" or, alternatively, as "dependable" and hardworking, are affect soaked.

31. I am indebted to Feldman and Steenbergen 2001 for highlighting the distinction between egalitarianism and humanitarianism, and developing indicators of both.

32. The correlation between the measures of Racial Prejudice and Positive Esteem for Blacks is –.44.

33. Coefficients for prejudice and positive esteem are only estimated because the quantity of interest is the total effect of each, indirect as well as direct. Both are very early in the causal chain, if not at the beginning, on the available evidence.

34. See Lelkes and Sniderman 2016.

35. March 15, 2016: Florida, 45.7 percent; Illinois, 38.8 percent; North Carolina, 42.3 percent; Missouri, 48 percent.

36. The survey was done by YouGov. RR1 and RR2 for Republicans were 39.7 and 4.8 percent.

37. Tesler and Sears's 2010 concept of "the two sides of racialization," operationalized by separating the two positive and the two negative indicators in the symbolic racism/racial resentment measure, is a candidate. Of the work that I am aware of, the most promising is Chudy 2015.

38. Sometimes this concept of prejudice goes under the heading of symbolic racism, sometimes under that of racial resentment. The arguments underpinning each, not to mention the measures of both, are interchangeable. For convenience, I'll use only one of the monikers, symbolic racism, but what I have to say applies equally to both. Quote from Kinder and Sanders 1996, p. 124.

39. The obvious explanation for the singular predictive power of measures of symbolic racism/racial resentment is that they simultaneously measure what they want to explain, positions on issues of race, and what they claim is doing the explaining, namely, symbolic racism or racial resentment. See Schuman 2000 and Carmines, Sniderman, and Easter 2011.

40. E.g., Sears 1988; Henry and Sears 2002; Sears and Henry 2005.

41. Figure 3.3 lists the meanings attributed to the concepts of symbolic racism/racial resentment in the temporal order in which they were

presented. It is worth noting that earlier ones regularly reappear in later work.

42. See, inter alia, Feldman and Huddy 2005; Hughes 1997; Sears, Van Laar, Carrillo, and Kosterman 1997; Sears, Henry, and Kosterman 2000; Kinder and Mendelberg 2000; Sniderman, Peri, de Figuerido, and Piazza 2000.

43. Kinder and Mendelberg 2000, p. 60; italics in original.

44. Kinder and Mendelberg 2000, p. 60.

45. Sears and Henry 2003, p. 264.

46. Sears 1988, p. 73.

47. The correlation between measures of symbolic racism and egalitarianism for white Americans for the 2012 ANES is –.35.

48. Kinder and Dale-Riddle 2012, p. 177; italics mine. Not the least puzzling thing is that although conceptual definitions of racial resentment/symbolic racism change radically over time, the operational definition is the same or so similar as to make no difference.

49. Kinder and Sears 1981, p. 416.

50. Sears and Henry 2003, p. 264.

51. Sears 1988, p. 74.

52. Sears and Henry 2003, p. 271.

53. Kinder and Sears 1981, p. 423.

CHAPTER 4. THE FEAR OF MASS POLITICS

1. Among the most influential: Dahl 1989; Stouffer 1967; McClosky 1964.

2. This section draws on the argument and analysis of Sniderman, Fletcher, et al. 1996, pp. 14–51, Ch. 2, "The Thesis of Democratic Elitism."

3. This section recapitulates McClosky 1964 and Dahl's 1989 classic analyses.

4. Quoted in McClosky 1964, p. 361.

5. Stouffer 1967, pp. 6–57.

6. Stouffer 1967, p. 42.

7. Stouffer 1967, p. 43, Table 4.

8. Stouffer 1967, p. 34.

9. Sniderman, Fletcher, Russell, and Tetlock 1996, Ch. 2.

10. McClosky and Brill 1983 devote a chapter demonstrating the

connection between ideology and political tolerance. See Ch. 7, pp. 274–335.

11. McClosky and Brill 1964, p. 292, Figure 7.2.

12. McClosky and Brill 1964, p. 294, Figure 7.3.

13. McClosky 1964, p. 374; italics added.

14. Throughout this section, I rely on Berinsky and Lenz 2014.

15. I follow Oshinsky 2005, pp. 108–110.

16. Oshinsky 2005, p. 109.

17. All the more reason not merely to read but also to study Oshinsky 2005.

18. E.g., judged by an overall measure of tolerance of nonconformists, two-thirds of community leaders scored high, compared with only one-third of the public at large. This is one of many examples that could be cited. Stouffer 1967, p. 46.

19. Oshinsky 2005.

20. Hofstadter 2008.

21. Polsby 1960.

22. Berinsky and Lenz 2014.

23. Berinsky and Lenz 2014, p. 385.

24. Berinsky and Lenz 2014, p. 388.

25. This section draws on Sniderman 1981.

26. Miller 1974, p. 951.

27. Beschloss 1972, p. 370.

28. Miller 1974.

29. See e.g., Weiner 2015.

30. Weiner 2015, p. 33, Table 6.

31. Weiner 2015, p. 33.

32. Dahl 1970, p. 4.

33. This section follows Schickler 2016.

34. Schickler 2016.

35. Their preferences have manifestly become more consistent, but that is not the same thing as becoming more extreme. See Fiorina 2008; Fiorina and Abrams 2008; Fiorina, Abrams, and Pope 2006.

36. It may be objected that the Democratic candidate's choice, taken individually, is inconsequential. But that is an argument against voting for this candidate whatever choice she makes.

37. This section draws on Sniderman and Stiglitz 2012. The bound-

ary conditions for weighting party more than candidates, in particular the Order Condition, are set out in Sniderman and Stiglitz 2012.

38. Hall 2016 has put on the table a quite new account of polarization, showing that the costs and benefits of holding office selectively disadvantage moderate potential candidates as against ideologically extreme ones.

39. Campbell et al. 1960, p. 133.

40. Bartels 2002, pp. 117–150.

41. Prior, Sood, and Khanna 2015.

42. Specifically, incentives for both correct answers and "don't know" eliminate 80 percent of the partisan gap. Bullock et al. 2015. See also Prior and Lupia 2008. It does not follow, I would emphasize, that the disposition to praise one's side and criticize the other is superficial. The appetitive and aversive feelings go deep.

43. Gaines et al. 2007, p. 964, Figure 4.

44. Kunda 1990.

45. Taber and Lodge 2006, p. 756.

46. Taber and Lodge 2006, p. 767.

47. Bayes's theorem sets out a formal algorithm for updating probabilities on the basis of new evidence.

48. Bullock 2009, p. 1122. Bullock sets the standard for clarity and depth of analysis of the problem of partisan "bias" and Bayesian updating.

49. Taber and Lodge 2006, p. 767.

EPILOGUE

1. It is particularly important to keep clear the distinction between the questions of the competence of citizens and the efficacy of elections as a mechanism of democratic control.

2. Achen and Bartels 2016 critique the "folk theory" on two broad fronts—populist and retrospective voting. The two share a theme—the judgment deficits of ordinary citizens. I will comment only on the issues on which I have presented empirical results, since I do not see the benefit of words about words.

3. Political realism, in the specific sense of tough-mindedness, has had a checkered career. In England, E. H. Carr was his generation's foremost exponent of realism, an honor bestowed without irony on a po-

litical analyst who got both Hitler and Stalin wrong. In America, realism is more nearly a synonym for cynicism. H. L. Mencken accordingly has become an honorary icon of political realism. Mencken was a curmudgeon of genius, but not a model for realism in the sense of accuracy of insight. There was, for one thing, his assault on the New Deal. There was, for another and more serious, his analysis of Germany. In his biography of Mencken, Manchester sums up Mencken's judgment. "As for the English and French, the idea of war between them and the Nazis was simply insane. No one wanted it; who would start it? And this constant mauling of Hitler as a fee-faw-fum and the Germs as a race of wolves: it wasn't true, and what purpose did it serve? The plain fact was that they were all fee-faw-fums, all wolves, and the sooner that was admitted the sooner some solution could be reached." A Mencken sample, written in 1939: "The one gang, led by Hitler and Mussolini, is trying to chase England and France out of the Mediterranean and all the territory east of the run of the Rhine and run both areas for themselves. The other gang, led by England France, is trying to build a doghouse around them to keep them in it." See Manchester 1967, p. 333.

4. E.g., myopic voting; punishing incumbents for events beyond their power to prevent or mitigate.

5. Achen and Bartels 2016, pp. 228–230.

6. For example, the social identity theory, developed by Henri Tajfel, is standardly distinguished from the self-categorization theory, developed by John Turner, a student of Tajfel's, and Turner's students; e.g., Turner and Reynolds 2010. For a discussion of some complexities of social identity and self-categorization theories that social identity theorists perceive political scientists have not taken into account, see Oakes 2002. For an insightful presentation of social identity theory from the perspective of a political scientist and a response to Oakes, see Huddy 2001, 2002.

7. Achen and Bartels 2016, p. 268; italics mine. I do not feel comfortable that I have fully understood their argument. Their major emphasis is the shallowness and incoherence of public opinion. See especially Chapter 2, pp. 21–51.

8. Achen and Bartels 2016, p. 268, italics in original.

9. Achen and Bartels 2016, p. 268. Note the plural "identities." For

Achen and Bartels, party identification need not be—indeed, in the illustrations of their approach is not—the relevant political identity.

10. See Hetherington and Rudolph 2015 for a path-discovering analysis identifying partisan-grounded distrust of government as a mechanism reinforcing gridlock.

11. Iyengar and Westwood 2015.

12. Sniderman and Stiglitz 2012.

13. See Ahn, Huckfeldt, and Ryan 2014; Mutz 2002, 2006; and Mutz and Mondak 2006. For negative consequences of uncivil disagreement, see Mutz 2007, 2015; Mutz and Reeve 2005; Dahl 1970.

14. Williams 2005, p. 58. See also Hampshire 2000.

15. Sniderman and Carmines 1997, pp. 91–140.

16. It may be worth noting that this claim of a winning coalition on race was made before the 2008 election, without, I would emphasize, any awareness that America was about to elect its first Black president.

APPENDIX

1. Downloaded from www.electionstudies.org.

2. ANES, "1987 Action Study," http://www.electionstudies.org /studypages/1987pilot/1987pilot.htm.

3. As suggested in Zaller 1992, p. 61, n. 10.

4. The content codes with asterisks appear in the Appendix Codebook provided by ANES at the website listed in n. 1.

Bibliography

Achen, Christopher H. 1975. "Mass Political Attitudes and the Survey Response." American *Political Science Review* 69(4):1218–1231.

———. 1982. *Interpreting and Using Regression.* Beverly Hills, CA: Sage.

Achen, Christopher H., and Larry M. Bartels. 2016. *Democracy for Realists.* Princeton, NJ: Princeton University Press.

Ahn, T. K., Robert Huckfeldt, and John Barry Ryan. 2014. *Experts, Activists, and Democratic Politics: Are Electorates Self-Educating?* New York: Cambridge University Press.

Alesina, Alberto, and Edward L. Glaeser. 2006. *Fighting Poverty in the U.S. and Europe.* New York: Oxford University Press.

Ansolabehere, Stephen, James M. Snyder, and Charles Stewart III. 2001. "Candidate Positioning in the U.S. House Elections." *American Journal of Political Science* 45:136–159.

Banting, Keith, and Will Kymlicka. 2013. "Is There Really a Retreat from Multiculturalism Policies? New Evidence from the Multiculturalism Policy Index." *Comparative European Politics* 11:577–598.

Bartels, Larry M. 1996. "Uninformed Votes: Information Effects in Presidential Elections." *American Journal of Political Science* 40: 194–223.

———. 2002. "Beyond the Running Tally: Partisan Bias in Political Perceptions." *Political Behavior* 24:117–150.

———. 2003. "Democracy with Attitudes." In Michael B. MacKuen and

George Rabinowitz, eds., *Electoral Democracy*, 48–82. Ann Arbor: University of Michigan Press.

———. 2005. "Homer Gets a Tax Cut: Inequality and Public Policy in the American Mind." *Perspectives on Politics* 3:15–31.

———. 2008. *Unequal Democracy*. Princeton, NJ: Princeton University Press.

———. 2013. "The Political Education of John Zaller." *Critical Review* 24(4):463–488.

Bawn, Kathleen, Martin Cohen, David Karol, Seth Masket, Hans Noel, and John Zaller. 2012. "A Theory of Political Parties: Nominations, Policy Demands, and American Politics." *Perspectives on Politics* 10: 571–597.

Berinsky, Adam J., and Gabriel S. Lenz. 2014. "Red Scare? Revisiting Joe McCarthy's Influence on 1950s." *Public Opinion Quarterly* 78: 369–391.

Beschloss, Michael R., ed. 1972. *Taking Charge: The Johnson White House Tapes, 1963–64*. New York: Touchstone.

Bishop, George F., Robert W. Oldendick, Alfred J. Tuchfarber, and Stephen E. Bennett. 1978. "The Changing Structure of Mass Belief Systems: Fact or Artifact?" *Journal of Politics* 40:781–787.

Blinder, Alan, and Mark Watson. 2016. "Presidents and the U.S. Economy: An Econometric Exploration." *American Economic Review* 106:1015–1045.

Boudreau, Cheryl. 2015. "Party Versus Principle: How Competing Parties and Frames Affect the Consistency Between Citizens' Values and Policy Views." Munro Lecture presented at Stanford University, Stanford, California, January 7.

Bowen, John R. 2008. *Why the French Don't Like Headscarves*. Princeton, NJ: Princeton University Press.

Brady, Henry E., and Paul M. Sniderman. 1985. "Attitude Attribution: A Group Basis for Political Reasoning." *American Political Science Review* 79:1061–1078.

Bullock, John G. 2009. "Partisan Bias and the Bayesian Ideal in the Study of Public Opinion." *Journal of Politics* 71:1109–1124.

———. 2011. "Elite Influence on Public Opinion in an Informed Electorate." *American Political Science Review* 105:496–515.

Bullock, John G., Alan S. Gerber, Seth J. Hill, and Gregory A. Huber.

2015. "Partisan Bias in Factual Beliefs About Politics." *Quarterly Journal of Political Science* 10:519–578.

Campbell, Angus, Philip E. Converse, Warren E. Miller, and Donald E. Stokes. 1960. *The American Voter.* New York: John Wiley and Sons.

Carmines, Edward G., and Geoffrey C. Layman. 1997. "Issue Evolution in Postwar American Politics: Old Certainties and Fresh Tensions." In Byron E. Shafer, ed., *Present Discontents: American Politics in the Very Late Twentieth Century,* 89–134. Chatham, NJ: Chatham House.

Carmines, Edward G., and James A. Stimson. 1989. *Issue Evolution: Race and the Transformation of American Politics.* Princeton, NJ: Princeton University Press.

Chaiken, Shelly. 1982. "Heuristic Versus Systematic Information Processing and the Use of Source Versus Message Cues in Persuasion." *Journal of Personality and Social Psychology* 39:752–766.

Chong, Dennis, and James N. Druckman. 2007. "Framing Public Opinion in Competitive Democracies." *American Political Science Review* 4:637–655.

Chong, Dennis, Herbert McClosky, and John Zaller. 1983. "Patterns of Support for Democratic and Capitalist Values in the United States." *British Journal of Political Science* 13:401–444.

Chudy, Jennifer. 2015. "Racial Sympathy in American Politics." Paper presented at the Annual Meeting of the American Political Science Association, San Francisco, California.

Cohen, Geoffrey L. 2003. "Party over Policy: The Dominating Impact of Group Influence on Political Beliefs." *Journal of Personality and Social Psychology* 85:808–822.

Cohen, Martin, David Karol, Hans Noel, and John Zaller. 2008. *The Party Decides: Presidential Nominations Before and After Reform.* Chicago: University of Chicago Press.

Conover, Pamela Johnston, and Stanley Feldman. 1981. "The Origins and Meaning of Liberal/Conservative Self-Identifications." *American Journal of Political Science* 25:617–645.

Converse, Philip E. 1964. "The Nature of Belief Systems in Mass Publics." In David E. Apter, ed., *Ideology and Discontent,* 206–261. New York: Free Press.

———. 1974. "Attitudes and Non-Attitudes: Continuation of a Dialogue." In Edward R. Tufte, ed., *The Quantitative Analysis of Social Problems*. Reading, MA: Addison-Wesley.

———. 2000. "Assessing the Capacity of Mass Electorates." *Annual Review of Political Science* 3:331–353.

Converse, Philip E., and Gregory B. Markus. 1979. "Plus ça change . . . : The New CPS Election Study Panel." *American Political Science Review* 73:32–49.

Crowder, George. 2013. *Theories of Multiculturalism*. Cambridge: Polity Press.

Dahl, Robert A. 1961. *Who Governs?* New Haven: Yale University Press.

———. 1970. *After the Revolution*. New Haven: Yale University Press.

Dobrzynk, Agnieska, and Andre Blais. 2008. "Testing Zaller's Reception and Acceptance Model in an Intense Election Campaign." *Political Behavior* 30:259–275.

Dollard, John. 1957. *Caste and Class in a Southern Town*. Madison: University of Wisconsin Press.

Druckman, James N. 2001. "The Implications of Framing Effects for Citizen Competence." *Political Behavior* 23:225–256.

Druckman, James N., Erik Peterson, and Rune Slothuus. 2013. "How Elite Partisan Polarization Affects Public Opinion Formation." *American Political Science Review* 107:57–79.

Eagly, A. H., and S. Chaiken. 1993. *The Psychology of Attitudes*. Orlando, FL: Harcourt Brace Jovanovich.

Ellis, Christopher, and James A. Stimson. 2012. *Ideology in America*. New York: Cambridge University Press.

Entmann, Robert M. 1993. "Framing: Toward Clarification of a Fractured Paradigm." *Journal of Communications* 43:51–58.

Erikson, Robert. 1979. "The SRC Panel Data and Mass Political Attitudes." *British Journal of Political Science* 9:89–114.

Feldman, Stanley. 1989. "Measuring Issue Preferences: The Problem of Response Instability." *Political Analysis* 1:25–26.

Feldman, Stanley, and Leonie Huddy. 2005. "Racial Resentment and White Opposition to Race Conscious Programs: Principle or Prejudice?" *American Journal of Political Science* 49:168–183.

Feldman, Stanley, and Marco Steenbergen. 2001. "The Humanitarian Foundation of Public Support for Social Welfare." *American Journal of Political Science* 45:658–677.

Fiorina, Morris P. 2008. "Polarization in the American Public: Misconceptions and Misreadings." *Journal of Politics* 70:542–555.

Fiorina, Morris P., and Samuel J. Abrams. 2008. "Political Polarization in the American Public." *Annual Review of Political Science* 11:563–588.

Fiorina, Morris P., with Samuel J. Abrams, and Jeremy C. Pope. 2005. *Culture War? The Myth of a Polarized America*, 2nd ed. New York: Pearson Longman.

Gaines, Brian J., James H. Kuklinski, Paul J. Quirk, Buddy Peyton, and Jay Verkuilen. 2007. "Same Facts, Different Interpretations: Partisan Motivation and Opinion on Iraq." *Journal of Politics* 69:957–974.

Gamson, William A., and Andre Modigliani. 1989. "Media Discourse and Public Opinion: A Constructionist Approach." *American Journal of Sociology* 95:1–37.

Gauchet, Marcel. 1997. "Right and Left." In Pierre Nora and Lawrence D. Krizman, eds., *Realms of Memory: Conflicts and Divisions*. New York: Columbia University Press.

Gibson, J. J. 1986. *An Ecological Theory of Ideological Consistency*. New York: Psychology Press.

Gilovich, Thomas, Dale Griffin, and Daniel Kahneman. 2002. *Heuristics and Biases: The Psychology of Intuitive Judgment*. New York: Cambridge University Press.

Goren, Paul. 2013. *On Voter Competence*. New York: Oxford University Press.

Greeley, Andrew, and Paul Sheatsley. 1971. "Attitudes Toward Racial Integration." *Scientific American* 223:13–19.

Green, Donald, Bradley Palmquist, and Eric Schickler. 2002. *Partisan Hearts and Minds*. New Haven: Yale University Press.

Grice, Paul. 1989. "Logic and Conversation." In *Studies in the Ways of Words*, 22–40. Cambridge, MA: Harvard University Press.

Hall, Andrew B. 2016. *Who Wants to Run? How the Devaluing of Political Office Drives Polarization*. Unpublished Manuscript.

Hampshire, Stuart. 2000. *Justice Is Conflict*. Princeton, NJ: Princeton University Press.

Henry, P. J., and David O. Sears. 2002. "The Symbolic Racism 2000 Scale." *Political Psychology* 23:253–283.

Hetherington, Marc J. 1991. "Resurgent Mass Partisanship: The Role of Elite Polarization." *American Political Science Review* 95:619–631.

Hetherington, Marc J., and Thomas J. Rudolph. 2015. *Why Washington Won't Work.* Chicago: University of Chicago Press.

Hofstader, Richard. 2008. *The Paranoid Style in American Politics and Other Essays.* New York: Vintage.

Huddy, Leonie. 2001. "From Social to Political Identity: A Critical Examination of Social Identity Theory." *Political Psychology* 22:125–156.

———. 2002. "Context and Meaning in Social Identity Theory: A Response to Oakes." *Political Psychology* 23:825–838.

Huddy, Leonie, and Stanley Feldman. 2009. "On Assessing the Political Effects of Racial Prejudice." *Annual Review of Political Science* 12: 423–447.

Hughes, Michael. 1997. "Symbolic Racism, Old-Fashioned Racism, and Whites' Opposition to Affirmative Action." In Steven A. Tuch and Jack K. Martin, eds., *Racial Attitudes in the 1990s,* 45–75. Westport, CT: Praeger.

Hurwitz, Jon, and Mark Peffley, eds. 1998. *Perception and Prejudice: Race and Politics in the United States.* New Haven: Yale University Press.

Hyman, Herbert H., and Paul B. Sheatsley. 1956. "Attitudes Toward Desegregation." *Scientific American* 195:35–39.

———. 1964. "Attitudes Toward Desegregation." *Scientific American* 211:16–23.

Iyengar, Shanto, Kyu Hahn, Christoper Dial, and Mahzarin R. Banaji. 2009. "Understanding Explicit and Implicit Attitudes: A Comparison of Racial Group and Candidate Preferences in the 2008 Election." Unpublished paper.

Iyengar, Shanto, and Nicholas A. Valentino. 2000. "Who Says What? Source Credibility as a Mediator of Campaign Advertising." In Arthur Lupia, Mathew D. McCubbins, and Samuel L. Popkin, eds., *Elements of Reason: Cognition, Choice, and the Bounds of Rationality,* 108–129. New York: Cambridge University Press.

Iyengar, Shanto, and Sean J. Westwood. 2015. "Fear and Loathing Across Party Lines: New Evidence on Group Polarization." *American Journal of Political Science* 59:690–707.

Jackman, Simon, and Paul M. Sniderman. 2002. "The Institutional Organization of Choice Spaces: A Political Conception of Political

Psychology." In Kristen Monroe, ed., *Political Psychology*. Mahway, NJ: Lawrence Erlbaum.

———. 2006. "The Limits of Deliberative Discussion: A Model of Everyday Political Arguments." *Journal of Politics* 68:272–283.

Jacoby, William G. 1988. "The Impact of Party Identification on Issue Attitudes." *American Journal of Political Science* 32:643–661.

Kahneman, Daniel. 2011. *Thinking Fast and Slow*. New York: Farrar, Straus and Giroux.

Kahneman, Daniel, and Amos Tversky. 2000. *Choices, Values and Frames*. New York: Cambridge University Press.

Kam, Cindy D. 2005. "Who Toes the Party Line? Cues, Values, and Individual Differences." *Political Behavior* 27:163–182.

Karol, David A. 2009. *Party Position Change in American Politics: Coalition Management*. New York: Cambridge University Press.

Khair, Tabish. 2015. *The New Xenophobia*. New York: Oxford University Press.

Kinder, Donald R. 1998. "Attitude and Action in the Realm of Politics." In Daniel Gilbert, Susan Fiske, and Gardner Lindzey, eds., *Handbook of Social Psychology*, 4th ed., 778–867. Hoboken, NJ: Wiley.

———. 2006. "Belief Systems Today." *Critical Review* 18:197–216.

Kinder, Donald R., and Allison Dale-Riddle. 2012. *The End of Race?* Chicago: University of Chicago Press.

Kinder, Donald R., and Nathan P. Kalmoe. 2008. "The Nature of Ideological Identification in Mass Publics: Meaning and Measurement." Paper presented at the annual meeting of the American Political Science Association, Boston, Massachusetts.

———. 2009. "The Nature of Ideological Identification in Mass Publics Part II: Formation and Consolidation." Paper presented at the annual meeting of the American Political Science Association, Toronto, Canada.

———. 2010. "The Nature of Ideological Identification in Mass Publics Part III: Consequences." Paper presented at the annual meeting of the Mid-West Political Science Association, Chicago, Illinois.

Kinder, Donald R., and Cindy D. Kam. 2009. *Us Against Them: Ethnocentric Foundations of American Opinion*. Chicago: University of Chicago Press.

Kinder, Donald O., and Tali Mendelberg. 2000. "Individualism Reconsidered." In David O. Sears, Jim Sidanius, and Lawrence Bobo, eds., *Racialized Politics*, 44–74. Chicago: University of Chicago Press.

Kinder, Donald R., and Lynn M. Sanders. 1996. *Divided by Color.* Chicago: University of Chicago Press.

Kinder, Donald R., and David O. Sears. 1981. "Prejudice and Politics." *Journal of Personality and Social Psychology* 40:414–431.

Klineberg, Otto. 1968. "Prejudice: The Concept." In D. Sills, ed., *Encyclopedia of the Social Sciences*, 12:439–448. New York: Macmillan.

Knight, Kathleen 1985. "Ideology in the 1980 Election." *Journal of Politics* 47:828–853.

Kunda, Ziva. 1990. "The Case for Motivated Reasoning." *Psychological Bulletin* 108:480–498.

Kymlicka, Will. 1995. *Multicultural Citizenship.* New York: Oxford University Press.

Kymlicka, Will, and Keith Banting. 2006. "Immigration, Multiculturalism, and the Welfare State." *Ethics and International Affairs* 20: 281–304.

Langer, Ellen, Arthur Blank, and Benzion Chanowitz. 1978. "The Mindlessness of Ostensibly Thoughtful Action: The Role of 'Placebic' Information in Interpersonal Interaction." *Journal of Personality and Social Psychology* 36:635–642.

Lau, Richard R., and David P. Redlawsk. 2001. "Advantages and Disadvantages of Cognitive Heuristics in Political Decision Making." *American Journal of Political Science* 45:951–971.

Lavine, Howard G., Christopher D. Johnson, and Marco R. Steenbergen. 2012. *The Ambivalent Partisan.* New York: Oxford University Press.

Leeper, Thomas J., and Rune Slothuus. 2016. "If Only Citizens Had a Cue: The Process of Opinion Formation over Time." Working paper, London School of Economics and Political Science/Aarhus University.

Lelkes, Yphtach, and Paul M. Sniderman. 2016. "The Ideological Asymmetry of the American Party System." *British Journal of Political Science* 46:825–844.

Lenz, Gabriel. 2009. "Learning and Opinion Change, Not Priming: Reconsidering the Priming Hypothesis." *American Journal of Political Science* 53:821–837.

———. 2012. *Follow the Leader.* Chicago: University of Chicago Press.

Levendusky, Matthew. 2009. *The Partisan Sort: How Liberals Became Democrats and Conservatives Became Republicans.* Chicago: University of Chicago Press.

Lewis, Charlton T. 1890. *An Elementary Latin Dictionary.* New York: American Book Company.

Lewis-Beck, Michael S., William G. Jacoby, Helmut Norpath, and Herbert F. Weisberg. 2008. *The American Voter Revisited.* Ann Arbor: University of Michigan Press.

Lippmann, Walter. 1922. *Public Opinion.* New York: Harcourt and Brace.

———. 1927. *The Phantom Public.* New York: Harcourt & Brace.

Lodge, Milton, and Charles S. Taber. 2013. *The Rationalizing Voter.* New York: Cambridge University Press.

Lupia, Arthur. 2016. *Uninformed.* New York: Oxford University Press.

Lupia, Arthur, Adam Seth Levine, Jesse O. Menning, and Gisela Sin. 2007. "Were Bush Tax Cut Supporters 'Simply Ignorant'? A Second Look at Conservatives and Liberals in 'Homer Gets a Tax Cut.'" *Perspectives on Politics* 5:761–772.

Lupia, Arthur, Mathew D. McCubbins, and Samuel L. Popkin. New York: Cambridge University Press.

Luskin, Robert C. 1987. "Measuring Political Sophistication." *American Journal of Political Science* 31:856–899.

Manchester, William. 1967. *Disturber of the Peace: The Life of H. L. Mencken.* New York: Harper.

Mattei, Paola, and Andrew S. Aguilar. 2016. *Secular Institutions, Islam and Education Policy: France and the U.S. in Comparative Perspective.* London: Palgrave Macmillan.

McClosky, Herbert. 1964. "Consensus and Ideology in American Politics." *American Political Science Review* 58:361–382.

McClosky, Herbert, and Alida Brill. 1983. *Dimensions of Tolerance.* New York: Russell Sage Foundation.

McClosky, Herbert, Paul J. Hoffmann, and Rosemary O'Hara. 1960. "Issue Conflict and Consensus Among Party Leaders and Followers." *American Political Science Review* 54:406–427.

McConnell, Christopher, Yotam Margalit, Neil Malhotra, and Matthew Levendusky. n.d. "The Economic Consequences of Partisanship in a Polarized Era."

McFadden, Daniel. 1999. "Rationality for Economists." *Journal of Risk and Uncertainty* 19:73–105.

McGraw, Kathleen, Milton Lodge, and Patrick Stroh 1990. "On-Line Processing in Candidate Evaluation: The Effect of Issue Order, Salience, Issue Importance and Sophistication." *Political Behavior* 12: 41–58.

McMahon, Christopher. 2009. *Reasonable Disagreement.* New York: Cambridge University Press.

Mill, John Stuart. 2008. *On Liberty and Other Essays.* Oxford: Oxford University Press.

Miller, Arthur H. 1974. "Political Issues and Trust in Government: 1965–1970." *American Political Science Review* 68:951–972.

Miller, Warren E., and J. Merrill Shanks. 1996. *The New American Voter.* Cambridge, MA: Harvard University Press.

Mutz, Diana C. 2002. "Cross-Cutting Social Networks: Testing Democratic Theory in Practice." *American Political Science Review* 96(2):111–126.

———. 2006. *Hearing the Other Side: Deliberative Versus Participatory Democracy.* New York: Cambridge University Press.

———. 2007. "Effects of 'In-Your-Face' Television Discourse on Perceptions of a Legitimate Opposition." *American Political Science Review* 101(4):621–635.

———. 2015. *In Your Face Politics: The Consequences of Incivility.* Princeton, NJ: Princeton University Press.

Mutz, Diana C., and Jeffery J. Mondak. 2006. "The Workplace as a Context for Cross-cutting Political Discourse." *Journal of Politics* 68(1):140–155.

Mutz, Diana C., and Byron Reeves. 2005. "The New Videomalaise: Effects of Televised Incivility on Political Trust." *American Political Science Review* 99(1):1–15.

Myrdal, Gunnar. 1944. *An American Dilemma.* New York: Harper and Bros.

———. 1973. "An American Dilemma: Has It Been Resolved?" In *Against the Stream,* 293–307. New York: Vintage Books.

Nelson, Thomas E., Rosalee A. Clawson, and Zoe M. Oxley 1997. "Media Framing of a Civil Liberties Controversy and Its Effect on Tolerance." *American Political Science Review* 91:567–584.

Nelson, Thomas E., and Donald R. Kinder. 1996. "Issue Frames and Group-Centrism in American Public Opinion." *Journal of Politics* 58:1055–1078.

Nie, Norman H., Sidney Verba, and John R. Petrocik. 1979. *The Changing American Voter.* Cambridge, MA: Harvard University Press.

Noel, Hans. 2013. *Political Ideologies and Political Parties in America.* Cambridge: Cambridge University Press.

Nolan, McCarty, Keith Poole, and Howard Rosenthal. 2006. *Polarized America.* Cambridge, MA: MIT Press.

Norris, Pippa, and Ronald Inglehart. 2003. "Islamic Culture and Democracy: Testing the 'Clash of Civilizations' Thesis." In Ronald Inglehart, ed., *Human Values and Social Change.* Leiden: Brill.

Oakes, Penelope. 2002. "Psychological Groups and Political Psychology: A Response to Huddy's 'Critical Examination of Social Identity Theory.'" *Political Psychology* 23:809–824.

O'Gorman, Hubert J. 1975. "Pluralistic Ignorance and White Estimates of White Support for Racial Segregation." *Public Opinion Quarterly* 39:313–333.

O'Gorman, Hubert J., with Stephen L. Garry. 1976. "Pluralistic Ignorance: A Replication and Extension." *Public Opinion Quarterly* 40: 449–458.

Oshinsky, David M. 2005. *A Conspiracy So Immense: The World of Joe McCarthy.* New York: Oxford University Press.

Peffley, Mark A., and Jon Hurwitz. 1985. "A Hierarchical Model of Attitude Constraint." *American Journal of Political Science* 29:871–889.

———. 1998. *Perception and Prejudice: Race and Politics in the United States.* New Haven: Yale University Press.

Petty, R. E., and J. T. Cacioppo. 1986. "The Elaboration Likelihood Model of Persuasion." In L. Berkowitz, ed., *Advances in Experimental Social Psychology,* 19:123–205. San Diego, CA: Academic Press.

Polsby, Nelson W. 1960 "Towards an Explanation of McCarthyism." *Political Studies* 8:250–271.

Poole, Keith T., and Howard Rosenthal. 1997. *Congress: A Political-Economic History of Roll Call Voting.* New York: Oxford University Press.

Prior, Markus, and Arthur Lupia. 2008. "Money, Time, and Political

Knowledge: Distinguishing Quick Recall from Political Learning Skills." *American Journal of Political Science* 52:168–182.

Prior, Markus, Gaurav Sood, and K. Khanna. 2015. *The Impact of Accuracy Incentives on Partisan Bias in Reports of Economic Perceptions.* Unpublished manuscript.

Rahn, Wendy M. 1993. "The Role of Partisan Stereotypes in Information Processing about Political Candidates." *American Journal of Political Science* 37:472–496.

Random House Unabridged English Dictionary. 1969. New York: Random House.

Raz, Joseph. 1986. *The Morality of Freedom.* Oxford: Oxford University Press.

Roberts, Gene, and Hank Klibanoff. 2006. *The Race Beat.* New York: Vintage Books.

Rosenberg, Morris, and Roberta G. Simmons. 1971. *Black and White Self-Esteem: The Urban School Child.* Washington, DC: American Sociological Association.

Ross, Lee. 1977. "The False Consensus Effect: An Egocentric Bias in Social Perception and Attribution Processes." *Journal of Experimental Social Psychology* 13:279–301.

Schickler, Eric. 2016. *Racial Realignment: The Transformation of American Liberalism, 1932–1965.* Princeton, NJ: Princeton University Press.

Schuman, Howard. 2000. "The Perils of Correlation, the Lure of Labels, and the Beauty of Negative Results." In David O. Sears, James Sidanius, and Lawrence Bobo, eds., *Racialized Politics: The Debate About Racism in America.* Chicago: University of Chicago Press.

Schuman, Howard, and John Harding. 1963. "Sympathetic Identification with the Underdog." *Public Opinion Quarterly* 27:230–241.

Sears, David O. 1988. "Symbolic Racism." In P. A. Katz and D. A. Taylor, eds., *Michael*, 53–84. New York: Plenum Press.

Sears, David O., and P. J. Henry. 2003. "The Origins of Symbolic Racism." *Journal of Personality and Social Psychology* 85:259–275.

———. 2005. "Over Thirty Years Later: A Contemporary Look at Symbolic Racism." *Advances in Experimental Social Psychology* 37:95–149.

Sears, David O., P. J. Henry, and R. Kosterman. 2000. "Egalitarian Values and Contemporary Racial Politics." In David O. Sears, James Sidanius, and Lawrence Bobo, eds., *Racialized Politics: The*

Debate About Racism in America, 75–117. Chicago: University of Chicago Press.

Sears, David O., Colette Van Laar, Mary Carrillo, and Rick Kosterman. 1997. "Is It Really Racism?" *Public Opinion Quarterly* 61:16–53.

Selznick, Gertrude J., and Stephen Steinberg. 1969. *The Tenacity of Prejudice: Anti-Semitism in Contemporary America.* New York: Harper and Row.

Sherif, M., M. S. Sherif, and R. E. Nebergall. 1965. *Attitude and Attitude Change.* Philadelphia: W. B. Saunders.

Simpson, G. E., and J. M. Inger. 1985. *Racial and Cultural Minorities: An Analysis of Prejudice and Discrimination*, 5th ed. New York: Plenum.

Slothuus, Rune. 2010. "When Can Political Parties Lead Public Opinion? Evidence from a Natural Experiment." *Political Communication* 27:158–177.

Sniderman, Paul M. 1981. *A Question of Loyalty.* Berkeley: University of California Press.

———. 2000. "Taking Sides: A Fixed Choice Theory of Political Reasoning." In Arthur Lupia, Mathew D. McCubbins, and Samuel L. Popkin, eds., *Elements of Reason: Cognition, Choice, and the Bounds of Rationality*, 67–84. New York: Cambridge University Press.

Sniderman, Paul M., and Edward G. Carmines. 1997. *Reaching Beyond Race.* Cambridge, MA: Harvard University Press.

Sniderman, Paul M., Pierangelo Peri, Rui de Figuerido, and Thomas Piazza. 2000. *The Outsider: Prejudice and Politics in Italy.* Princeton, NJ: Princeton University Press.

Sniderman, Paul M., Michael Bang Petersen, Rune Slothuus, and Rune Stubager. 2014. *Paradoxes of Liberal Democracy: Islam, Western Europe and the Danish Cartoon Crisis.* Princeton, NJ: Princeton University Press.

Sniderman, Paul M., and Thomas Piazza. 1993. *The Scar of Race.* Cambridge, MA: Harvard University Press.

Sniderman, Paul M., and Edward J. Stiglitz. 2012. *The Reputational Premium: A Theory of Party Identification and Spatial Reasoning.* Princeton, NJ: Princeton University Press.

Sniderman, Paul M., and Philip E. Tetlock. 1986a. "Symbolic Racism: Problems of Political Motive Attribution." *Journal of Social Issues* 42:129–150.

———. 1986b. "Reflections on American Racism." *Journal of Social Issues* 42:173–188.

Sniderman, Paul M., Philip E. Tetlock, James M. Glaser, Donald Phillip Green, and Michael Hout. 1989. "Principled Tolerance and American Political Values." *British Journal of Political Science* 19:25–46.

Sniderman, Paul M., and Sean M. Theriault. 2004. "The Structure of Political Argument and the Logic of Issue Framing." In Willem Saris and Paul M. Sniderman, *Studies in Public Opinion*, 133–165. Princeton, NJ: Princeton University Press.

Snyder, James M., Jr., and Michael M. Ting. 2002. "An Informational Rationale for Political Parties." *American Journal of Political Science* 46:90–110.

Soames, Scott. 2005. *Philosophical Analysis in the Twentieth Century*, vol. 2: *The Age of Meaning*. Princeton, NJ: Princeton University Press.

Southern, David W. 1987. *Gunnar Myrdal and Black-White Relations*. Baton Rouge: Louisiana State University Press.

Squire, Peverill, and Smith, Eric R. A. N. 1988. "The Effect of Partisan Information on Voters in Nonpartisan Elections." *Journal of Politics* 50:169–179.

Stimson, James A. 1975. "Belief Systems: Constraint, Complexity, and the 1972 Election." *American Journal of Political Science* 19:393–417.
———. 2004. *Tides of Consent*. New York: Cambridge University Press.

Stone, Walter J., and Matthew K. Buttice. 2010. "Voters in Context: The Politics of Citizen Behavior." In Jan E. Leighley, ed., *The Oxford Handbook of American Elections and Political Behavior*, 555–576. Oxford: Oxford University Press.

Stouffer, Samuel A. 1967. *Communism, Conformity, and Civil Liberties*. New York: John Wiley & Sons.

Sullivan, John L., James E. Piereson, George E. Marcus, and Stanley Feldman. 1979. "The More Things Change, the More They Stay the Same: The Stability of Mass Belief Systems." *American Journal of Political Science* 23:176–186.

Taber, Charles, and Milton Lodge. 2006. "Motivated Skepticism in the Evaluation of Political Beliefs." *American Journal of Political Science* 50:755–769.

Taylor, Charles. 1994. "The Politics of Recognition." In Amy Gutmann, ed., *Multiculturalism: Examining the Politics of Recognition.* Princeton, NJ: Princeton University Press.

Taylor, D. Garth, Paul B. Sheatsley, and Andrew Greeley. 1978. "Attitudes Toward Racial Integration." *Scientific American* 238:42–49.

Taylor, Shelley E., and Susan Fiske. 1978. "Salience, Attention, and Attribution: Top of the Head Phenomena." *Advances in Experimental Social Psychology* 11:249–288.

Tesler, Michael, and David O. Sears. 2010. *Obama's Race: The 2008 Election and the Dream of a Post-Racial America.* Chicago: University of Chicago Press.

Tetlock, Philip E. 1984. "Cognitive Style and Political Belief Systems in the British House of Commons." *Journal of Personality and Social Psychology: Personality Process and Individual Differences* 46:365–375.

Thaler, Richard. 2015. *Misbehaving: The Making of Behavioral Economics.* New York: W. W. Norton.

Tomz, Michael, and Paul M. Sniderman. 2005. "Brand Names and the Organization of Mass Belief Systems." Unpublished paper.

Turner, John C., and Katherine J. Reynolds. 2010. "The Story of Social Identity." In T. Postmes and N. Branscombe, eds., *Rediscovering Social Identity: Core Sources,* 13–32. New York and Hove: Psychology Press.

Weiner, Tim. 2015. *One Man Against the World: The Tragedy of Richard Nixon.* New York: Henry Holt.

Williams, Bernard. 2005. *In the Beginning Was the Word.* Princeton, NJ: Princeton University Press.

———. 2007. *Ethics and the Limits of Philosophy.* Oxford: Routledge.

Young, Iris Marion. 1995. *Justice and the Politics of Difference.* Princeton, NJ: Princeton University Press.

Zaller, John. 1992. *The Nature and Origins of Mass Opinion.* Cambridge: Cambridge University Press.

Zaller, John, and Stanley Feldman. 1992. "A Simple Theory of the Survey Response: Answering Questions Versus Revealing Preferences." *American Journal of Political Science* 36:579–616.

Index

top-down politics, 9, 19–25
"top-of-the-head" model, 9–19, 40, 41
transgender rights, 110, 111
Trump, Donald, 98–99, 139
trust in government, 1–2, 120–122
Turner, John, 162 n. 6

understanding, 24–25, 38
unemployment, 35–36, 49, 128

values: of American Creed, 81; as anchors, 34; democratic, 6, 80, 107, 110–111, 115, 125; issue framing and, 30–31; as justifications, 30; social, 59, 61; traditional, 65, 66, 102–106

Vietnam War, 2, 121
Voting Rights Act (1965), 81

Watergate scandal, 122
Weathermen, 121
welfare spending. *See* social welfare
Williams, Bernard, 139
wiretapping, 112

xenophobia, 83
Xerox experiment, 34–35

yielding, 24–25, 38, 39–40

Zaller, John, 9–10, 11–19